Contents

KU-022-424

Demystifying ISO 9000

Demystifying ISO 9000

Gerard W. Paradis
Fen Small
International Quality Systems

ADDISON-WESLEY
An imprint of Addison Wesley Longman, Inc.
Reading, Massachusetts • Harlow, England • Menlo Park, California
Berkeley, California • Don Mills, Ontario • Sydney
Bonn • Amsterdam • Tokyo • Mexico City

Many of the designations used by manufacturers and sellers to distinguish their products are claimed as trademarks. Where those designations appear in this book and Addison-Wesley was aware of a trademark claim, the designations have been printed with initial capital letters.

The publisher offers discounts on this book when ordered in quantity for special sales. For more information, please contact:

Corporate, Government, and Special Sales Group
Addison Wesley Longman, Inc.
One Jacob Way
Reading, Massachusetts 01867

Library of Congress Cataloging-in-Publication Data
Paradis, Gerard W., 1942–
    Demystifying ISO 9000 / Gerard W. Paradis, Fen Small, and
    Information Mapping Team ISO.
        p.   cm.
    Includes index.
    ISBN 0-201-63490-2 (pbk, : alk. paper)
    1. ISO 9000 Series Standards. I. Small, Fen. II. Information
Mapping, Inc. Team ISO. III. Title.
TS156.6.P37   1996
658.5'62– – dc20   96-13795
                                               CIP

This manual has been developed using the standards of the Informational Mapping methodology. Information Mapping is a registered trademark.

Information Mapping is a registered service mark of Information Mapping, Inc.
Info-Map is a registered trademark of Information Mapping, Inc.

International Quality Systems is a registered trademark of International Quality Systems, Inc.

6 7 8 9 1011 MA   01 00 99 98
6th Printing December 1998

Chapter 8   Site Preparation

Preface

Introduction

In March of 1993, Team ISO of Information Mapping, Inc., published the first edition of *Demystifying ISO 9000: Information Mapping's Guide to the ISO 9000 Standards*. The book's aim was to help readers better understand the five basic ISO 9000 Standards. It was also meant to provide a proven path forward to certification to one of the three ISO 9000 Quality System Models (ISO 9001, 9002, or 9003).

The response to the guide has been overwhelmingly positive. *Demystifying ISO 9000: Information Mapping's Guide to the ISO 9000 Standards* became an instant best-seller and the reviews came in raving about the usability of the text. Over 100 organizations purchased multiple copies and distributed them to their ISO coordination teams.

The 1994 version

The 1994 version of *Demystifying ISO 9000: Information Mapping's Guide to the ISO 9000 Standards* was created to respond to customer demands and to parallel the revisions to the ISO 9000 Standards published on July 1, 1994.

In addition to covering the changes in the Standard in 1994, this guide was totally revised and now includes chapters on

- planning,
- gap analysis,
- corrective action,
- document structure,
- document and records control, and
- certification preparation.

Information Mapping and ISO

The idea for using the principles of Information Mapping to document quality systems for conformance to the ISO 9000 Standards evolved from a series of seminars held by Information Mapping, Inc., for quality assurance personnel at Eastman Kodak Company starting in 1991.

Continued on next page

Preface, Continued

**Information
Mapping
and ISO,**
(continued)

The foundation for these first quality documentation seminars was the Information Mapping course, *Developing Procedures, Policies and Documentation*, first developed by Robert Horn in 1977. Since 1991, Information Mapping, Inc., has worked to improve quality system documentation at a number of other organizations and to expand the quality system content of seminars for those seeking ISO 9000 certification.

Using this guide

This document is to be used in conjunction with, not as a substitute for, the ISO 9001 International Standard Model for Quality Assurance in Design/Development, Production, Installation, and Servicing.

The ISO 9000 series of Standards is published in the United States as the American National Standards Institute/American Society for Quality Control Q9000 Series.

**Use a registered
agency**

This document provides interpreted information of the ISO 9000 Standard. If your organization is seeking certification for compliance with the ISO 9000 Standards, contact an auditor accredited by a registered agency.

Thanks

We wish to acknowledge the help of many people:

- The core, original membership of Team ISO at Information Mapping, including Dan Morgan, Steve Gousie, and Kathy Fast.
- Terrance Johnston of Eastman Kodak Company, whose sponsorship made the initial series of Information Mapping for ISO 9000 possible.
- Andrew Strawhand of Andrew Strawhand Associates for his review and suggestions on "opportunities for improvement" in the initial draft of the first edition.
- James DiNitto for countless recommendations in this second edition.

Continued on next page

Preface, Continued

Thanks,
(continued)

In addition, we would like to thank many on the staff of Information Mapping, Inc., for their help in ensuring that this document conforms to the principles of the Information Mapping methodology.

We are also grateful to the many attendees of our ISO 9000 documentation seminars who have continued to add their ideas to this effort.

Special thanks

We want to give special thanks to Anne Brown, who researched, edited, and revised this version. Her high level of editing skill, creativity, and hard work is evident in the pages that follow. There would be no book without Anne's contribution.

Gerard Paradis
Fen Small

Update to Preface

Intoduction

In January of 1997, Information Mapping, Inc. formed a new company, International Quality Systems, Inc. (IQS) to focus on its growing ISO 9000 business. IQS' mission is to provide our clients with the knowledge and tools needed to document and implement their quality systems.

Benefits

A well-documented information Mapped quality system, certified or compliant to ISO 9000, can give your company the consistency it needs to avoid roadblocks to success resulting in

- reduction in variability
- fewer mistakes
- less waste
- improved operational efficiency, and
- cost savings

Seven-module approach

IQS can clear the way to consistency in your company with our proven, comprehensive, Seven-Module approach to certification. All of our clients have achieved certification the first time with our training and consulting help. In fact, when you use our approach, we guarantee your success, or we will pay for your reaudit! Contact us today at 1-888-ISO-7677 or at www.isomap.com.

James R. DiNitto
President and CEO

Chapter 1

Introduction to the ISO 9000 Certification Process

Overview

Introduction

This chapter introduces the ISO 9000 Standards, ISO 9000 concepts, and the ISO quality system certification process.

ISO 9000 series Standards

This diagram illustrates relationship of the ISO 9000 series Standards.

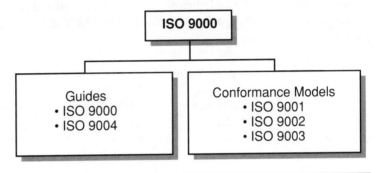

In this chapter

This chapter contains the following topics:

Topic	See Page
The ISO 9000 Standards	2
What Is a *Quality System*?	4
Understanding Quality Audits	6
Overview of the Certification Process	8

The ISO 9000 Standards

Introduction
There are five Standards in the basic ISO 9000 series. These five Standards are either conformance models or guides.

- A *conformance model* is a Standard to which your organization must conform in order to be certified.
- A *guide* is a set of recommendations concerning the establishment of an effective quality system in order to be certified in one of the conformance models.

Conformance models and guides
The table below lists the three conformance models and the two guides of the basic ISO 9000 series.

Type of Standard	Name of Standard	Description of Standard
Conformance Model	ISO 9001	Quality assurance in design/development, production, installation, and servicing.
	ISO 9002	Quality assurance in production, installation, and servicing.
	ISO 9003	Quality assurance in final inspection and test.
Guide	ISO 9000	Guidelines for selection and use of the standards on quality management, quality system elements, and quality assurance.
	ISO 9004	Guidelines for quality management and quality system elements.

Continued on next page

The ISO 9000 Standards, Continued

**Sections
of the
Standard**

This table lists the twenty sections of the Standard and identifies which ISO 9000 conformance model covers these sections.

Note: ISO 9003 usually has reduced requirements for the sections it covers.

This section . . .	Is Covered in this ISO Standard.		
	9001	*9002*	*9003*
4.1 Management Responsibility	✓	✓	✓
4.2 Quality System	✓	✓	✓
4.3 Contract Review	✓	✓	✓
4.4 Design Control	✓		
4.5 Document and Data Control	✓	✓	✓
4.6 Purchasing	✓	✓	
4.7 Control of Customer Supplied Product	✓	✓	✓
4.8 Product Identification and Traceability	✓	✓	✓
4.9 Process Control	✓	✓	
4.10 Inspection and Testing	✓	✓	✓
4.11 Control of Inspection, Measuring, and Test Equipment	✓	✓	✓
4.12 Inspection and Test Status	✓	✓	✓
4.13 Control of Nonconforming Product	✓	✓	✓
4.14 Corrective and Preventive Action	✓	✓	✓
4.15 Handling, Storage, Packaging, Preservation, and Delivery	✓	✓	✓
4.16 Control of Quality Records	✓	✓	✓
4.17 Internal Quality Audits	✓	✓	✓
4.18 Training	✓	✓	✓
4.19 Servicing	✓	✓	
4.20 Statistical Techniques	✓	✓	✓

What Is a Quality System?

Definition

A *quality system* is the organizational structure, responsibilities, procedures, processes, and resources needed to implement quality management. It should only be as comprehensive as needed to meet quality objectives.

What gets certified?

Your quality system must conform to the ISO 9000 Standard that your organization selects. It is the *quality system* that becomes certified (registered) during the certification process.

Quality system terms

The table below describes the key terms found in the ISO 9000 Standards relating to a quality system.

Term	Description
product	The material or service provided. Applies in the Standard to • incoming material/service, • in-process product/service, and • finished product/service.
supplier	Your organization.
subcontractor	Your supplier.
customer	The organization that receives your product/service.

Quality system relationships

The diagram below represents the relationship between

• the subcontractor,
• the supplier (your organization),
• your customer, and
• the product.

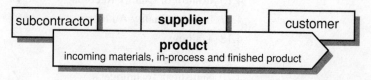

Continued on next page

What Is a Quality System? Continued

ISO verb meanings

There are two main verbs used throughout the ISO 9000 Standard that relate to your quality system. These verbs are described in the table below.

THE verb . . .	MEANS that compliance is . . .	AND is found only in the . . .
shall	required	conformance models.
should	recommended	guides.

Understanding Quality Audits

Introduction   Your organization may undergo several types of audits:

- first-party audits,
- second-party audits, and
- third-party audits.

Definition of audit   An *audit* is an evaluation of your quality system and documentation.

First-party audits   The *first-party audit* is an internal quality system audit performed by the supplier (your organization) on its own quality system.

Second-party audits   The *second-party audit* is a quality system audit performed by your customer on the supplier (your organization).

Third-party audits   The *third-party audit* is a quality system audit performed by the auditor on the supplier (your organization) in order to achieve certification for one of the ISO 9000 Standards.

The third-party auditor must be independent of both your customer and the supplier (your organization). Third-party audits *cannot* be performed by the customer or the supplier.

Continued on next page

Understanding Quality Audits, Continued

What the auditor looks for

The graphic below describes what the auditor looks for when performing a third-party audit.

What Does the Auditor Look For?

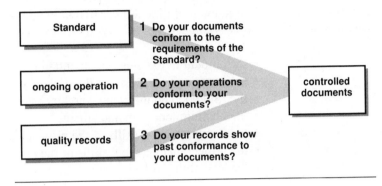

Overview of the Certification Process

Time to complete
The typical certification process may last from *twelve* to *eighteen months*.

Factors affecting completion
The amount of time it takes to complete the certification process can depend on several factors, such as:

- the amount of existing documentation,
- the complexity and size of the organization,
- the ISO 9000 conformance model chosen for certification,
- the commitment of management,
- the documentation skills of the project teams,
- the project management skills of the project teams, and
- the availability of certification auditors.

Stages in the process
This table describes the stages of the certification process.

Stage	Name	What Happens
1	Strategic Planning	Management: • displays strong commitment to the certification effort, • selects a registrar, • selects a conformance model for which organization may seek certification, • forms a project team, • establishes a timeline, and • assesses training needs regarding ISO 9000 and organizational background.
2	Gap Analysis	Corrective action teams: • evaluate the existing quality system against the selected conformance model, and • evaluate the documentation against the quality system and the selected conformance model.

Continued on next page

Overview of the Certification Process, Continued

**Stages
in the
process**
(continued)

Stage	Name	What Happens
3	Corrective Action	Corrective action teams institute changes in quality system as identified in Stage 2.
4	Documentation and Records	Corrective action teams: • implement a document structure and control system • institute a control of quality records process • revise documents, as necessary, and • provide training about changes, additions, and other topics as identified in Stage 1.
5	Implementation	Management: • implements and monitors all changes in the quality system • ensures all gaps identified in Stage 2 are closed, and • maintains records of all changes.
6	Pre-Certification Audit	Pre-assessment auditor ensures that all operations and documentation are according to the selected conformance model.
7	Registrar Documentation Review	Registrar reviews quality manual (and any other requested documents) as advance organizer to the organization and the supporting documentation.
8	Site Preparation	Management prepares organization for the registrar and certification audit.
9	Certification Audit	Registrar reviews quality system and documentation to determine if quality system meets the selected conformance model and can be certified as such.

Overview of the Certification Process, Continued

Road to certification

This diagram illustrates the road to ISO certification.

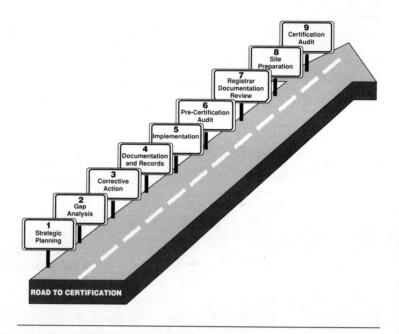

Coming next

Chapter 2 provides descriptions of each section of the ISO 9001 conformance model to help your organization down the road to certification.

Chapter 2

The Twenty Sections of ISO 9001

Overview

Purpose

This chapter discusses each of the twenty sections of the ISO 9001 Standard. ISO 9002 contains nineteen of the twenty sections and ISO 9003 contains sixteen of the twenty sections (usually with reduced requirements.)

Note: Refer to the pages titled "The ISO 9000 Standards" in Chapter 1 to see what sections are required for your selected conformance model.

How we cover each section

This table shows the primary subjects that this chapter covers for each section of ISO 9001.

Label	Description
Requirements	The primary requirements called for in this section of the ISO 9001 Standard.
What this means	Further clarification of the requirement(s).
Required documents and records	Specific information requirements for your controlled documents and quality records for this section of the Standard.
Auditor questions	Typical questions an auditor might ask for this section.

Overview, Continued

4.1 Management Responsibility

Your organization's management shall provide for

- **a quality policy,**
- **assignment of responsibility and authority to personnel,**
- **resources for identification and verification,**
- **appointment of a management representative, and**
- **a management review for the suitability and effectiveness of your quality system.**

What this means

The Standard requires management to take an active and leading role in the development, implementation, and maintenance of each of the five requirements.

Each of the five requirements is discussed below or on the following pages.

Quality policy

Your management, with executive responsibility for quality, develops and maintains a quality policy showing

- quality objectives,
- management's commitment to quality,
- the policy's relevance to organizational goals, and
- customer needs and expectations.

Management ensures that all personnel in the organization understand, implement, and maintain this policy.

Responsibility and authority

Your management, with executive responsibility for quality, documents the personnel makeup to show

- individual responsibility,
- lines of authority, and
- relationship among personnel.

Continued on next page

4.1 Management Responsibility, Continued

Responsibility and authority (continued)

Special attention needs to be given to personnel assigned to product, process, and quality system problem solving, as well as to verification, prevention, and control of nonconformity.

Resources

Your management provides adequate resources and trained personnel for

- management;
- performance of work; and
- verification, including internal quality audits.

Management representative

Your management, with executive responsibility for quality, assigns a management member who, regardless of other responsibilities

- ensures that the quality system meets the requirements of the Standard, and
- reports quality system performance to management.

Management review

Your management conducts a periodic management review of your quality system for suitability and effectiveness. This review might include:

- results of internal audits,
- customer reactions or complaints,
- major or repetitive product nonconformances, and
- corrective/preventive actions.

Continued on next page

Required documents and records

This table shows the information required in controlled documents and quality records for this section of the Standard.

FOR ...	INCLUDE information on ...
controlled documents	• management policy, objectives, and commitment to quality; • responsibility, authority, and relationship of all personnel affecting quality; • in-house verification activities; and • process and procedures for management review for suitability and effectiveness.
quality records	proof of ongoing management reviews of your quality system's suitability and effectiveness, including corrective/preventive action taken.

Auditor questions

These are typical questions an auditor might ask for this section of the Standard.

Quality Policy

- What is your quality policy?
- How does management show commitment to quality?
- How do you ensure that your quality policy is understood and implemented throughout the organization?

Responsibility and Authority

- How do you identify personnel who manage, perform, or verify work affecting quality?
- How are responsibilities, authority, and relationships documented?
- How has the responsibility been defined for initiating action on preventing product nonconformance?

Continued on next page

Auditor questions
(continued)

Resources for Identification and Verification

- How are verification requirements and responsibilities defined?
- How are audits performed by personnel independent of those having direct responsibility for the work being performed?

Management Representative

- Who is the management representative responsible for ensuring that requirements of the Standard are implemented and maintained?
- How often does the management representative provide a review for management?

Management Review for Suitability and Effectiveness

- How often is a management review held?
- What sources are used for these reviews?
- What records of these reviews are maintained?

4.2 Quality System

Your organization shall

- **plan, establish, maintain, and document your quality system to ensure that your product and/or service conforms to specified requirements;**

- **provide an outline of the documentation structure and reference to immediate supporting documents in a quality manual; and**

- **provide quality plans.**

What is a
quality plan?

The Standard does not define a quality plan, nor does it go into any detail about what is required in a quality plan.

You should consider developing a quality plan for each of your products, services, and/or projects within your quality system. Where groups of products or services are similar, they might be included under a single quality plan.

What this means

These requirements may be seen as part of a four-stage process as shown in the table below and described in more detail on the following pages.

Stage	Name	What Your Organization Does
1	Quality system conformance to requirements	Ensures that your quality system conforms with the requirements of the Standard.
2	Quality system documentation	Prepares appropriate quality system documentation.
3	Quality plan documentation	Prepares appropriate documented quality plans for products, processes, and/or projects within the quality system.

Continued on next page

What this means
(continued)

Stage	Name	What Your Organization Does
4	Implementation	Implements the quality system, its documentation, and appropriate quality plans.

Stage 1—
Quality system
conformance
to requirements

Stage 1 is the quality planning of your quality system. It ensures that your quality system conforms to all of the appropriate requirements in each of the twenty sections of the ISO 9001 Standard.

During quality planning, consider, as appropriate:

- identification and acquisition of production resources and skills needed to achieve required quality;
- ensuring compatibility of
  - product design,
  - production process,
  - product installation and servicing, and
  - inspection and testing;
- ensuring quality control capability for inspection and testing;
- identification of measurement requirements requiring capability exceeding that of current known technology soon enough to develop capability;
- identification of suitable verification at appropriate stages in the product production;
- definition of product and process specifications.

Stage 2—
Quality system
documentation

Stage 2 is the documentation of your quality system. The Standard calls for documentation based on the

- complexity of your production process,
- skills needed, and
- existing training of personnel.

Continued on next page

Stage 2—
Quality system
documentation
(continued)

Documentation includes

- a quality manual showing an outline of the structure of your documentation and reference to supporting procedures, and
- procedures showing your
  - processes,
  - work instructions in support of these processes, and
  - identification of required records.

Reference: Guidance on the preparation of a quality manual is found in ISO 10013: *Guidelines for Developing Quality Manuals*.

Note: See Chapters 5 through 7 in this manual for more information on approaches to documenting your quality system.

Stage 3—
Quality plan
documentation

Stage 3 is the documentation of appropriate quality plans for

- individual or related groups of products,
- processes, and
- projects.

Note: Quality plans need not repeat the content found in your quality system documents. Quality plans may, in whole or part, be a reference to appropriate quality system documents.

Stage 4—
Implementation

Stage 4 is the implementation of your quality system, its documentation, and any appropriate quality plans.

Continued on next page

Required documents and Records

This table shows the information required in your controlled documents and quality records for this section of the Standard.

FOR ...	INCLUDE information on ...
controlled documents	• the quality manual; • quality plans for products, processes, and/or projects; • supporting procedures describing your processes; and • supporting procedures describing work instructions and required records.
quality records	any records required by your documentation (see other section requirements).

Auditor questions

These are typical questions an auditor might ask for this section of the Standard.

Quality Planning

• How are controls, processes, inspection equipment, and personnel resources identified and put in place to achieve required quality?
• How is the need for changes in quality control determined?
• How are measurement requirements determined?
• How are standards of acceptability determined?
• How is compatibility of product, process, installation, servicing, inspection, and documentation determined?

Quality Manual Supporting Documentation

• Where is your documented quality manual?
• Where does the quality manual contain
  • the quality policy,
  • an outline of the document structure,

Continued on next page

4.2 Quality System, Continued

Auditor questions
(continued)

- major policies in support of the sections and subsections of the Standard, and
  - reference to supporting documentation?
- How have all processes such as training, internal auditing, document control, and the like been documented in supporting documents?
- How is the need for additional procedures determined?
- How do procedures include requirements for records?

Quality Plans

How do quality plans cover products, processes, and/or projects as appropriate?

Implementation

- How is the quality system being operated?
- Is the quality system operated according to the documentation?

4.3 Contract Review

Requirements **Your organization shall review each contract or accepted order with your customer to ensure that**

- **customer requirements are adequately defined, and**
- **your organization has the capability to meet these needs.**

What this means You need to be able to demonstrate through records that you have reviewed requests for quotations, contracts, or accepted orders between your organization and the customer for your products and/or services.

Note: This customer normally is outside your company, but may be another organization within your company.

What to review These are items in the contract that you need to review.

Contract Element	Things to Review
What product is needed?	Product specifications
How many?	• total quantity of product, • quantity in each shipment, and • quantity in each lot.
When, where, and how?	• dates, • location, • method of transit, and • packaging for shipment.
Responsibilities?	• product verification, • nonconforming product, and • contract review or amendment.
Acceptance procedures	• what they are, • who does them, and • when they are done.

Continued on next page

4.3 Contract Review, Continued

**Required
documents
and records**

This table shows the information required in your controlled documents and quality records for this section of the Standard.

FOR . . .	INCLUDE information on . . .
controlled documents	• contract review process and procedures, • product and/or service specifications, • contract or order with your customer, and • acceptance procedures.
quality records	• proof of review, including resolution of any deviations, and • evidence of your capability to meet contracts.

Auditor questions

These are typical questions an auditor might ask for this section of the Standard.

• What is the documented process for contract review?
• What responsibilities for the contract review process are defined for the customer and supplier?
• How are customer requirements (specifications) defined and documented?
• What is the process for defining customer requirements?
• Where orders are taken verbally, what is the process for ensuring that order requirements are agreed to?
• How is capability to meet customer requirements determined?
• How are differences between customer and supplier resolved?
• What contract review records are maintained?

4.4 Design Control

Requirement | **Your organization shall control and verify the design of its product to ensure that it meets specified requirements.**

What this means | You need to have

- a design control process with responsibilities assigned to qualified personnel and adequate resources,
- defined interfaces between different design process groups,
- routine communications between groups,
- records maintained of these communications, and
- revisions of design and development plans, as necessary.

Design control process | This table describes a typical design control process.

Stage	Name	What Your Design Control Team Does
1	Design and development planning	Completes plans. This includes • description of each design, development, verification, and validation activity; • identification of responsibilities and resources for each activity; • identification of interfaces between design/development groups; and • establishment of communications links. *Note*: Plans need to be updated as necessary as the design evolves.
2	Design input	• Develops design; • reviews for adequacy; and • resolves incomplete, ambiguous, or conflicting requirements. *Note*: Design requirements also include any applicable statutory and regulatory requirements.

Continued on next page

Design control process (continued)

Stage	Name	What Your Design Control Team Does
3	Design output	• Ensures compliance with design input such as • acceptance criteria, • applicable regulatory requirements, • crucial safety characteristics, and • proper product functioning. • Reviews design output records before release.
4	Verification and validation	• Verifies that design output meets input requirements, and • validates that final product conforms to defined user needs and/or requirements.

Diagram of the design control process

The design control process is usually in the form of a cycle that

• allows for continual improvement through each cycle pass,
• is driven at each stage by the needs of the customer, and
• provides feedback to the customer.

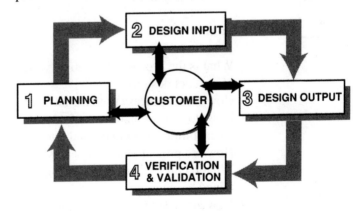

Continued on next page

4.4 Design Control, Continued

Required documents and records

This table shows the information required in your controlled documents and quality records for this section of the Standard.

FOR . . .	INCLUDE information on design . . .
controlled documents	• control process, responsibilities, resources and procedures; • input requirements (specifications); • output; • verification process, responsibilities, resources, and procedures; • validation process, responsibilities, resources, and procedures; and • change process, responsibilities, and procedures.
quality records	• group interface communications, • input review and approval, • output verification results, • reviews, and • change with verification results and change approval.

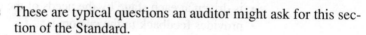

Auditor questions

These are typical questions an auditor might ask for this section of the Standard.

Planning

• What is the process for control, verification, and validation of product design?
• How is this process used for all product design?
• How do project plans identify design and development responsibilities, resources, and interfaces?
• How are project plans revised as design evolves?
• What records of project and design changes are maintained?
• How are design and development verification and validation activities identified?

Continued on next page

4.4 Design Control, Continued

- How are verification and validation personnel qualified and provided with adequate resources?
- What are the interfaces between design and development groups?
- How are communications handled between groups?
- What records are maintained of these communications?

Design Input

- How are product and project requirements identified?
- How are requirements reviewed for adequacy?
- How are conflicting requirements resolved?
- How are representatives of all design functions represented at periodic design reviews throughout the process?

Design Output

How does design output

- meet design input,
- contain reference to acceptance criteria,
- conform to appropriate regulatory requirements, and
- identify design characteristics crucial to safe, proper product function?

Design Verification and Validation

- How are criteria for design verification and validation identified?
- Who has responsibility for verification and validation?
- How does verification and validation determine that design output matches design input?
- How are changes and modifications recorded?

4.5 Document and Data Control

Requirement

Your organization shall control all your quality system documents and data to ensure availability of documented information to those requiring it.

Definitions

Documents and data contain approved information to ensure that your quality system policies, processes, and procedures are carried out in the proper manner. Although the Standard does not define data, these could include data sheets, computer software, and product standards.

Quality records contain information on what has happened in the quality system in the past.

Note: For every event, documents and data come before it, and quality records come after it.

Caution: Quality record control is not a part of this section. It is covered in Section 4.16 of the Standard.

What the requirement means

You need to show that you have a document and data control process. This should include provision for accessibility and reviews, revisions, approvals, and dispositions.

You need to show control of any documents and data supplied to you by an external source and used in your quality system. Examples could include standards, software for equipment operation, or customer specifications.

Accessibility

Accessibility includes

• a *document reference index* (like a document master list) that is accessible to organization personnel and shows the most current revision of each controlled document or data sheet;

Continued on next page

Accessibility
(continued)

- *organization* of your controlled documents and data sheets in a structure allowing easy access to information and forming a trail between documents or data sheets with related information;

- controlled documents and data sheets *formatted* to allow easy access to information;

- controlled documents and data sheets in *hard copy, electronic, or other media* accessible to those requiring them; and

- *obsolete documents* and data sheets removed to preclude their accidental use.

Note: Any obsolete documents retained for record purposes immediately become quality records.

Review, revision, approval, and disposition

Review, revision, approval, and disposition includes

- new and revised documents and data sheets *reviewed and approved* by authorized personnel with subject matter expertise for the information;

- reviewers and approvers having access as necessary to *supporting reference material*;

- *immediate disposition* of all obsolete documents and data sheets;

- changes indicated in revised documents and data sheets or in some form of *change notice*; and

- *periodic review* of each document and data sheet.

Note: Periodic review is not specifically called for in the Standard, but most auditors feel it is a critical part of document control.

Continued on next page

4.5 Document and Data Control, Continued

Required documents and records

This table shows the information required in your controlled documents and quality records for this section of the Standard.

FOR ...	INCLUDE information on ...
controlled documents	• document and data control process and procedures, • document and data sheet master list or similar means of document indexing, • lists of those approving documents and data sheets, and • document and data sheet review schedule.
quality records	• copy distribution lists, • document and data sheet review results, • individual document and data sheet background information, and • identification of nature of change.

Auditor questions

These are typical questions an auditor might ask for this section of the Standard.

• What is your process for controlling quality system documents and data sheets?
• Who approves release of documents and data sheets?
• How do personnel have access to documents and data sheets they require?
• How are obsolete documents and data sheets accounted for?
• How are changes reviewed and approved by the same functions that reviewed and authorized the original documents and data sheets?
• How are changes identified?
• What document and data sheet master list or similar listing is readily available to personnel? Where is it?

4.6 Purchasing

Requirement   **Your organization shall ensure that purchased product conforms to specified requirements.**

What this means   You need to establish a purchasing process ensuring that purchased products coming into your quality system meet specified requirements. The purchasing process includes subcontractor evaluation, purchasing data, and verification at the subcontractor level.

Note: ISO 8402: *Quality Management and Quality Assurance—Vocabulary* defines *product* as including hardware, software, processed material, and/or service.

Subcontractor evaluation   The subcontractor evaluation process includes:

- evaluation and selection of subcontractors based on their ability to meet your requirements, with selection criteria based on
  - the type of product and
  - previously demonstrated capability and performance;
- evaluation of subcontractor quality system effectiveness;
- definition of type and extent of supplier control over the subcontractor, based on the
  - impact of the subcontractor's product on your product quality,
  - the subcontractor's previously demonstrated capability, and
  - results of previous quality audits; and
- maintaining a list of acceptable subcontractors.

Purchasing data   The purchasing data process includes review and approval of purchase orders for

- identification and description of product ordered;
- inspection requirements;
- quantity and delivery;

Continued on next page

4.6 Purchasing, Continued

Purchasing data
(continued)

- requirements for approval of product, process, and/or personnel;
- the appropriate ISO Standard to be applied; and
- requirements for supplier or customer product verification and/or product release at the subcontractor's site.

Verification at the subcontractor site

Either you or your customer may choose to conduct product verification and/or product release at the subcontractor's site. Verification by the customer does not absolve you of responsibility for effective control of quality at your subcontractor's site.

Required documents and records

This table shows the information required in your controlled documents and quality records for this section of the Standard.

FOR ...	INCLUDE information on ...
controlled documents	• purchasing process and procedures, • list of acceptable subcontractors, and • product specifications.
quality records	• subcontractor capability, including effectiveness of quality system controls, • selection of subcontractors, • periodic subcontractor review results, • purchasing data and contract, and • purchasing data review and approval.

Auditor questions

These are typical questions an auditor might ask for this section of the Standard.

- What is the documented process for ensuring that incoming material conforms to specifications?
- How are subcontractors selected?
- How are acceptable subcontractors documented?
- How is the performance of subcontractors reviewed?

Continued on next page

4.6 Purchasing, Continued

Auditor questions
(continued)

- Where on your purchase orders do you clearly describe
  - product ordered,
  - inspection requirements,
  - quantity and delivery requirements,
  - approval requirements,
  - appropriate ISO Standard to be applied, and
  - requirements for supplier or customer verification and/or release at the subcontractor's site (if appropriate)?
- How are purchase orders reviewed and authorized prior to release?

4.7 Control of Customer-Supplied Product

Requirement	**Your organization shall provide for verification, storage, and maintenance of customer-supplied product provided for incorporation into your product.**

What this means	Your customer becomes both your customer and your subcontractor when supplying you with product that is incorporated into your product.

Example: A customer supplies its corporate logo emblem for attachment to your product.

You need to ensure that responsibilities for quality on the customer-supplied product are well defined.

Responsibilities   This table shows responsibilities for supplier and customer.

Organization	Responsibilities

supplier	• Ensures that the product supplied to you is
	  • suitable for its purpose;
	  • protected in storage, handling, and use while in your quality system; and
	• reports to the customer if product supplied to you is lost, damaged, or otherwise found unsuitable at any time in your process.

customer (and subcontractor)	Ensures the quality of the product supplied to you.

Continued on next page

4.7 Control of Customer-Supplied Product, Continued

Required documents and records

This table shows the information required in your controlled documents and quality records for this section of the Standard.

FOR ...	INCLUDE information on ...
controlled documents	• verification process and procedures, • storage process and procedures, • maintenance process and procedures, and • nonconformance process and procedures.
quality records	• product lost, damaged, or unsuitable for use, and • verification results.

Auditor questions

These are typical questions an auditor might ask for this section of the Standard.

• What is the documented process for verification, storage, and maintenance of customer-supplied product?
• If customer-supplied product is lost, damaged, or unsuitable, how is this reported back to the customer?

4.8 Product Identification and Traceability

Requirement

Your organization shall provide any necessary identification and traceability of incoming materials, in-process product, and finished product.

Definition

This table defines and shows a graphic example of identification and traceability.

Term	Definition	Graphic Example
identification	Ability to separate two or more materials or products.	PRODUCT A PRODUCT B PRODUCT C PRODUCT D
traceability	Ability to separate a material or product by individual batch, lot, or unit.	PRODUCT A PRODUCT B PRODUCT C LOT 1 LOT 2 LOT 3

What this requirement means

You need to be able to demonstrate an ability to identify each of your products. Traceability is required only if specified in the contract, but may be advisable if lot tracking is important to your process.

Need for identification

There is always a need for product identification, but there may not always be a need to mark or segregate the product physically.

When the intended user can identify the product by common knowledge, sight, feel, or some other sense, the supplier and customer may agree that further identification is not necessary.

Continued on next page

Need for traceability

Traceability may be needed:

- when separation of product where age or shelf life may be important,
- when control of incoming material is necessary,
- when the subcontractor requests it,
- to segregate nonconforming product,
- to test status determination,
- for release of finished product,
- when customer requires it,
- when required by regulatory requirement, and
- as an aid for material resource management.

Required documents and records

This table shows the information required in your controlled documents and quality records for this section of the Standard.

FOR . . .	INCLUDE information on . . .
controlled documents	• product and lot identification process and procedures, and • product lists.
quality records	• listings of incoming material batch, lots, or units, and • listings of your product batches, lots, or units.

Auditor questions

These are typical questions an auditor might ask for this section of the Standard.

- What is the documented process for identification and traceability?
- How is product identified during all stages of production, delivery, and installation?
- When required, how are individual products or batches uniquely identified to provide traceability?
- What records are maintained for product identification and traceability?
- How long are these records maintained?

4.9 Process Control

Requirement

Your production, installation, and servicing processes are operated under controlled conditions.

What this means

You need to ensure that your production, installation, and servicing processes are operated under controlled conditions. This includes

- necessary documented procedures;
- use of suitable equipment;
- suitable working environment;
- compliance with reference
  - standards,
  - codes, and
  - quality plans and/or documented procedures;
- monitoring and control of process and product characteristics;
- approval of processes and equipment;
- standards for representative product or material samples; and
- suitable maintenance of equipment to ensure continuing process capability (preventive maintenance).

Special processes

A *special process* is one where the results of the process cannot be verified by later inspection and testing of the product.

Special processes require one or more of the following:

- pre-qualification of process capability and equipment,
- use of qualified operators, and
- continuous monitoring and control of key process characteristics.

Continued on next page

4.9 Process Control, Continued

Required documents and records

This table shows the information required in your controlled documents and quality records for this section of the Standard.

FOR ...	INCLUDE information on ...
controlled documents	• process and procedures for product • control, • monitoring, • change approval, and • maintenance; • work instructions; • reference standards, codes, and quality plans; and • representative material or product samples.
quality records	• process change approvals; • qualification approvals of special processes, their equipment, and personnel, as appropriate; • process monitoring results; and • process maintenance.

Auditor questions

These are typical questions an auditor might ask for this section of the Standard.

Note: Questions on special processes apply only where product results cannot be tested after the process. All auditor questions also apply to special processes.

All Processes

- How are each of the following processes that affect product quality controlled?
  - production processes?
  - installation processes?
  - servicing processes?
- What procedures are used to control each process?
- How is the need for a procedure determined?

Continued on next page

4.9 Process Control, Continued

- What ensures that process and installation equipment meet "fitness for use?"
- What additional standards or codes (health, safety, environmental) need to be complied with?
- What critical process characteristics consistent with product quality requirements have been identified?
- How are workmanship criteria affecting product quality identified, monitored, and maintained?
- What is the equipment maintenance process used to ensure continuing process capability?

Special Processes

- How are special processes identified?
- How are special processes monitored?
- What special requirements drive the process?
- What records are maintained for special processes, equipment, and personnel?

4.10 Inspection and Testing

Requirements   **Your organization shall ensure that**

- **incoming product is verified for conformance to specified requirements,**
- **in-process product is inspected and tested as necessary, and**
- **finished product is verified as conforming to specified requirements prior to release.**

What this means   You need to have an inspection and testing process that ensures quality of the product throughout your quality system. This process is documented in the quality plan and/or in the quality system documents.

This table shows the three primary stages for the inspection and testing process.

Stage	Name	What Your Organization Ensures
1	Receiving inspection and testing	Incoming product conforms to specified requirements. This includes • inspection or verification, and • holding until verified, or controlling until verified. *Note*: The extent of receiving inspection and testing is based on the amount of control at the subcontractor's site and the recorded evidence of past conformance.
2	In-process inspection and testing	Product in-process conforms to specified requirements. This includes • identification and inspection of product • monitoring of the process, and • holding or positively controlling product until tests are completed.
3	Final inspection and testing	Finished product conforms to specified requirements. This includes • completion of all required tests and conformance to specified requirements, and • release of product only after tests are complete.

**Required
documents
and records**

This table shows the information required in your controlled documents and quality records for this section of the Standard.

FOR . . .	INCLUDE information on . . .
controlled documents	• incoming product tests or verification process and procedures, • test process and procedures for in-process product, • test process and procedures for process monitoring, and • process and procedures for product final inspection.
quality records	• incoming product test results or verification, • in-process product test results, • results of process monitoring affecting product, and • final inspection and testing test results, with inspection authority responsible for release of product.

Auditor questions

These are typical questions an auditor might ask for this section of the Standard.

Documents and Records

• What is the documented process for inspection and testing?
• What are the documented test methods used in this process?
• Where does the quality plan or documented final inspection process require that all specified inspection and tests be completed, and product meet specified requirements?
• Where do inspection and test records clearly show that all tests were completed and released product met specified requirements?
• Where do the final inspection records show the inspection authority responsible for release of product?

Continued on next page

Receiving Inspection and Testing

- How is incoming product tested or verified to ensure conformance to specified requirements?
- How is the extent of receiving inspection based on the level of control and records of prior conformance provided by the subcontractor?
- If incoming material is used prior to conformance verification, how is it identified to allow possible recall or replacement?

In-Process Inspection and Testing

- How is in-process testing in conformance with quality system procedures?
- How do process monitoring and control methods ensure product conformance?
- What happens to product until all required tests have been completed?
- Where product is not held, how is product identified for possible recall?

Final Inspection and Testing

- How does final inspection ensure product conforms to specified requirements?
- Where is product held until all required test results are available?

4.11 Control of Inspection, Measuring, and Test Equipment

Requirements

Your organization shall

- **control, calibrate, and maintain inspection, measuring, and test equipment and software used in your quality system to demonstrate the conformance of product to specified requirements; and**
- **ensure that measurement uncertainty is known and consistent with the required measurement capability.**

What this means

You need a calibration process that ensures that your inspection, measuring, and test equipment and software have the capability consistently to provide the specified measurement requirements.

Note: ISO 10012: *Quality Assurance Requirements for Measuring Equipment* provides additional input on calibration.

Verification and calibration process

A typical verification and calibration process would include the stages shown in this table.

Stage	Your team ...	This includes ...
1	identifies measurement requirement.	the accuracy required.
2	selects test equipment and software.	the equipment and software abilities to provide test measurement required.
3	verifies test equipment and software.	the capability to perform measurement at required accuracy and precision.
4	provides for protection of inspection equipment and software.	• environmental conditions; • handling, preservation, and storage; and • safeguards against unauthorized adjustment or modification.

Continued on next page

4.11 Control of Inspection, Measuring, and Test Equipment, Continued

Verification and calibration process (continued)

Stage	Your team . . .	This includes . . .
5	documents the equipment calibration and software verification process and procedures.	• checking methods, • acceptance criteria, and • equipment calibration and software verification schedules.
6	calibrates equipment and verifies software.	• adhering to schedule, and • completing equipment calibration and software verification.
7	indicates software verification and equipment calibration status.	• tagging or stamping test equipment and software, and • recording software verification and hardware calibration.

Calibration traceability

Each item of test equipment needs to be calibrated against certified test equipment having a known valid relationship to nationally recognized standards, such as the National Institute of Standards and Technology (NIST). Where no nationally recognized standard exists, the basis of the calibration needs to be identified.

Validity of test results

For equipment found to be out of calibration or software found to be no longer capable of verifying product acceptability, the validity of test results needs to be checked on the product tested. This usually means reviewing and verifying all test results after the last acceptable calibration of equipment or verification of software.

Continued on next page

Required documents and records

This table shows the information required in your controlled documents and quality records for this section of the Standard.

FOR . . .	INCLUDE information on . . .
controlled documents	• required measurements and their accuracy; • identification of all inspection, measuring, and test equipment and software affecting product quality; • the National Standard or other basis for calibration; • calibration process and procedures; • software verification process and procedures; • action to be taken when results for equipment calibration or software are unsatisfactory; and • verification and calibration schedule.
quality records	• equipment calibration and software verification results, and • validity of previous inspection and test results when test equipment is found to be out of calibration or software is not verified.

Auditor questions

These are typical questions an auditor might ask for this section of the Standard.

Measurement and Accuracy

• How are required product measurements identified?
• How are measurement accuracy requirements identified?

Inspection Equipment and Software

• How is inspection equipment and software selected?
• What is the process for verifying inspection equipment and software prior to use?

Continued on next page

4.11 Control of Inspection, Measuring, and Test Equipment, Continued

Auditor questions
(continued)

- How are environmental conditions controlled to ensure inspection equipment and software provide accurate readings?
- How is inspection equipment and software handled and stored?
- How is inspection equipment and software safeguarded against unauthorized adjustment or modification?
- How is inspection equipment and software affecting the quality of product identified?

Calibration of Equipment and Verification of Software

- How is equipment calibration and software verification scheduled?
- How is calibration done for each item of inspection equipment and how is verification done for each item of inspection software?
- What are the calibration acceptance limits for each item of inspection equipment?
- How is verification status recorded?
- How are calibrations traceable to a National Standard?
- If calibrations are not traceable to a National Standard, what is the basis for calibration?
- Are all calibrations current?
- How is inspection equipment identified as to calibration status?
- How is software identified as to verification status?
- What is the process for verifying the test results of test equipment found to be beyond calibration limits or software not capable of verifying product quality?

4.12 Inspection and Test Status

Requirement   **Your organization shall ensure identification of inspection and test status of product throughout production, installation, and servicing.**

What this means   You need to be able to identify the inspection and test status of product throughout your production, installation, and servicing. This ensures that only the product passing the required inspections and tests, or released under an authorized concession, is released.

Test status indicators   Ways to indicate test status might include

- labels, tags, or stamps on individual product or batches;
- production status cards;
- storage in an identified location;
- inspection and test records; and
- material management software programs.

Required documents and records   This table shows the information required in your controlled documents and quality records for this section of the Standard.

FOR . . .	INCLUDE information on . . .
controlled documents	• responsibility for review and release of product, and • inspection and test status process and procedures.
quality records	• inspection and test results, and • releasing authority for conforming product.

Continued on next page

4.12 Inspection and Test Status, Continued

Auditor questions These are typical questions an auditor might ask for this section of the Standard.

- How is product inspection and test status shown?
- How is this identification maintained throughout your quality system?
- How is releasing authority identified and recorded?

4.13 Control of Nonconforming Product

Requirement   **Your organization shall ensure that nonconforming product is prevented from unintended use or installation.**

What this means   You need a process for controlling nonconforming incoming material, in-process product, or finished product. The table shows the five stages of a typical nonconforming product process.

Stage	Name	What Your Team Does
1	Identification	Identifies nonconforming product.
2	Evaluation	Evaluates extent of nonconformance. *Note*: The investigation and corrective action for the cause of the nonconformance is covered in the next section of the Standard, 4.14 Corrective and Preventive Action.
3	Segregation	Segregates the nonconforming product either physically or through marking.
4	Notification	Notifies all affected parties.
5	Disposition	Dispositions nonconforming product through • rework to meet the specified requirements, • acceptance by concession with or without repairs, • re-grading for alternative applications, or • rejects or scrap. *Note*: Repaired or reworked product requires re-inspection.

Continued on next page

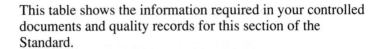

4.13 Control of Nonconforming Product, Continued

Required documents and records

This table shows the information required in your controlled documents and quality records for this section of the Standard.

FOR . . .	INCLUDE information on . . .
controlled documents	• responsibility for review and authority for disposition of nonconforming product, • control of nonconforming product process and procedures, • re-inspection procedures, and • agreement in contract on need for concession on use or repair.
quality records	• nonconformance investigation results and disposition action, • re-inspections of repaired or reworked product, • notification to interested parties, and • any acceptances by concession agreements.

Auditor questions

These are typical questions an auditor might ask for this section of the Standard.

• What is the process for ensuring that nonconforming product is prevented from unintended use or installation?
• How is nonconforming product identified?
• Who is responsible for the evaluation of nonconforming product?
• How is nonconforming product segregated?
• How are affected parties notified promptly?
• How is the proposed use of repaired or reworked product reported to the customer for agreement?
• How is reworked or repaired product re-inspected?
• How is rejected or scrapped product dispositioned promptly?
• What is the process for releasing product under an authorized concession?

4.14 Corrective and Preventive Action

Requirements

Your organization shall

- **investigate the cause of nonconforming product and consider corrective action needed to prevent recurrence, and**
- **analyze your quality system to detect and eliminate potential causes of nonconforming product.**

What this means

It is not enough just to control nonconforming product. You need a

- *corrective action process* to ensure that the cause of any nonconformity is eliminated to prevent recurrence, and
- *preventive action process* to detect and eliminate potential causes of nonconforming product *before* it occurs.

Corrective action process

This table shows the stages of the corrective action process.

Stage	Name	What Your Team Does
1	Nonconformance identification	Identifies nonconformance through • receipt of customer complaint, or • report of product nonconformity.
2	Cause investigation	Investigates the cause of the nonconformity relating to product, process, or quality system.
3	Corrective action	Determines the corrective action needed to eliminate the cause of the nonconformity.
4	Control application	Applies controls to ensure that corrective action is implemented and effective.

Continued on next page

4.14 Corrective and Preventive Action, Continued

Preventive action process

This table shows the stages of the preventive action process.

Stage	Name	What Your Team Does
1	Potential cause identification	Identifies • processes that affect product quality, • concessions, • audit results, • quality records, • service reports, and • customer complaints.
2	Potential cause investigation	Investigates the potential cause of nonconformities.
3	Preventive action	Determines the preventive action needed to eliminate the potential cause of nonconformities.
4	Control application	• Reviews change with management, • revises documents, • trains personnel, • implements change, and • applies controls to ensure preventive action is implemented and effective.

Required documents and records

This table shows the information required in your controlled documents and quality records for this section of the Standard.

FOR . . .	INCLUDE information on . . .
controlled documents	• corrective action process and procedures, • preventive action process and procedures, and • customer complaint process and procedures.
quality records	• customer complaints, • customer concessions, • corrective action investigation results, and • monitoring of corrective or preventive action for effectiveness.

Continued on next page

4.14 Corrective and Preventive Action, Continued

Auditor questions

These are typical questions an auditor might ask for this section of the Standard.

- What is the documented process for corrective action?
- What is the documented process for preventive action?
- How does your corrective action process include identification of the cause of the nonconforming product and action to prevent recurrence?
- How does the preventive action process include analysis of the quality system, quality records, customer complaints, and service reports?
- How are corrective and preventive actions made?
- How are corrective and preventive actions checked for effectiveness?
- How do the corrective and preventive processes ensure that documents are changed as a result of corrective or preventive action?

4.15 Handling, Storage, Packaging, Preservation, and Delivery

Requirement	**Your organization shall provide adequate handling, storage, preservation, packaging, and delivery of your product to ensure that it meets specified requirements.**

What this means	Handling, storage, preservation, and packaging requirements apply to

- incoming materials to your process,
- in-process product, and
- finished product.

Delivery requirements apply to protection of finished product after release. Where specified in the contract, product protection during delivery may extend to receipt by your customer.

Things to consider	The table lists potential items to consider for each of the requirements of this section. Your actual needs will depend on your product and process.

Requirement	Things to consider . . .
Handling	• product protection through the use of pallets, specialized containers, and work platforms; • design and adjustment of conveyors and other automated transfer systems; • operator training and awareness of product protection needs; and • proper operation of loaders and other vehicles.
Storage	• adequate space and facilities, • cleanliness, • environment (temperature, humidity), • security, and • identification and traceability.

Continued on next page

Things to consider (continued)

Requirement	Things to consider ...
Packaging	• protection, identification, and traceability in • unit protection, and • shipping cases.
Preservation	• environment (temperature, humidity), and • segregation or some other means of identification and traceability.
Delivery	• product protection after release until point in distribution process agreed to in contract, including: • delivery method, • environment (temperature, humidity), • in-transit delays and storage, and • security and cleanliness of delivery.

Required documents and records

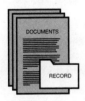

This table shows the information required in your controlled documents and quality records for this section of the Standard.

FOR ...	INCLUDE information on ...
controlled documents	• handling requirements, process and procedures; • storage requirements, process and procedures, to include receipt and dispatch authorization; • preservation requirements, process and procedures; • packaging requirements, process, and procedures; • packaging labels and shipping container formats; and • delivery requirements, process, and procedures.
quality records	• storage dates (as needed), • storage condition verification results, • results of calibration of storage control equipment (as needed),

Continued on next page

4.15 Handling, Storage, Packaging, Preservation, and Delivery, Continued

Required documents and records (continued)

FOR . . .	INCLUDE information on . . .
quality records	• expiration dating (as needed), • delivery dates (as needed), • verification results on mode of delivery, and • calibration results of mode of delivery (as needed).

Auditor questions

These are typical questions an auditor might ask for this section of the Standard.

- How is product handled to prevent damage?
- How are storage areas secured, and do they prevent damage and deterioration?
- Where product shelf life dictates, is the first in, first out principle used?
- How is product preserved during production?
- What provisions are made for product protection after final inspection and test?
- How does packaging protect product in expected distribution?
- How does packaging provide for any necessary expiration dating?
- How does packaging provide for adequate identification of the product?
- How is product delivery a part of the contract?

4.16 Control of Quality Records

Requirements

Your organization's control of quality records process shall ensure that your quality records demonstrate that

- **your quality system operates effectively, and**
- **required product quality is achieved.**

What this means

You need a process for control of quality records. With this process you make records accessible to those who need them, while minimizing deterioration and damage and preventing loss.

Note: Quality records need to be legible and identifiable to each product.

Control of quality records process

This table shows the stages of the control of quality records process.

Stage	Name	What Your Team Does
1	Identification	Identifies individual record and retention needs.
2	Collection	Identifies responsibility for record collection.
3	Indexing	Develops an indexing structure that provides an access trail.
4	Filing	Files quality records where access is easy during the frequent-review part of the individual record life.
5	Storage	Stores quality records in less accessible bulk storage during the required archival part of the individual record life.
6	Disposition	Disposes of individual record when it is no longer needed.

Continued on next page

4.16 Control of Quality Records, Continued

**Required
documents
and records**

This table shows the information required in your controlled documents and quality records for this section of the Standard.

FOR . . .	INCLUDE information on . . .
controlled documents	• need for specific records (these would be part of procedures called for in other sections), • process and procedures for control of quality records, and • required records index and retention schedule.
quality records	• records management reviews, and • records dispositions.

Auditor questions

These are typical questions an auditor might ask for this section of the Standard.

- What is the process for control of quality records?
- Who is assigned responsibilities for the control of quality records process?
- What subcontractor records are a part of the quality records?
- How are records legible and traceable to product?
- How do indexing and filing of records allow easy retrieval?
- How do records storage facilities minimize deterioration and damage and prevent loss?
- What are retention times for each type of quality record?
- How are retention times adhered to?
- Where called for in the contract, are records available for evaluation by the customer?

4.17 Internal Quality Audits

Requirement

Your organization's internal quality audit plan shall verify that your quality activities and related results meet requirements, and determine the effectiveness of your quality system.

What this means

You need to have an internal quality audit plan (internal auditing process) that provides input to management on the conformance and effectiveness of your quality system. The output of this process will serve as input to the corrective action process of Section 4.14 and the management review process of Section 4.1 of the Standard.

Internal audit process

This table describes a typical internal audit process.

Stage	Responsibility	Description
1	Quality system management	Develops audit plan.
2	Quality system management	Schedules audits on the basis of status and importance of the activity.
3	Auditor	Audits organization, including effectiveness of any previous corrective action.
4	Auditor	Submits audit report to management of the area audited.
5	Quality system management	Reviews noncompliances.
6	Quality system management	Takes timely corrective action on noncompliances.

Note: Additional guidance on quality system audits is in ISO 10011: *Guidelines for Auditing Quality Systems*. This three-part Standard covers auditing, auditor qualifications, and audit program management.

Continued on next page

4.17 Internal Quality Audits, Continued

Required documents and records

This table shows the information required in your controlled documents and quality records for this section of the Standard.

FOR ...	INCLUDE information on ...
controlled documents	• annual internal audit plan, including audit schedule, • internal audit process and procedures, and • list of qualified auditors.
quality records	• audit reports, and • management audit review and corrective action.

Auditor questions

These are typical questions an auditor might ask for this section of the Standard.

- What is the internal quality audit plan (internal quality audit process)?
- How many internal quality audits are scheduled and conducted?
- How do these audits check conformance to requirements and effectiveness?
- How are auditors qualified?
- How are auditors independent of those having direct responsibility for the area being audited?
- How are audit results recorded and brought to the attention of personnel responsible for the area audited?
- What corrective action is taken on deficiencies found in the audit?
- How do auditors ensure that corrective action, as a result of prior audits, has been effective and has eliminated deficiencies?
- How are results of audit reports used in the management review?

4.18 Training

Your organization shall identify training needs and train personnel to meet these needs.

What this means Employees need to know what to do in order to do their jobs effectively.

This means you need to develop a training process based on your quality system job needs and the level of individual personnel knowledge.

Continued on next page

4.18 Training, Continued

Training process The diagram below shows a typical training process for new employees.

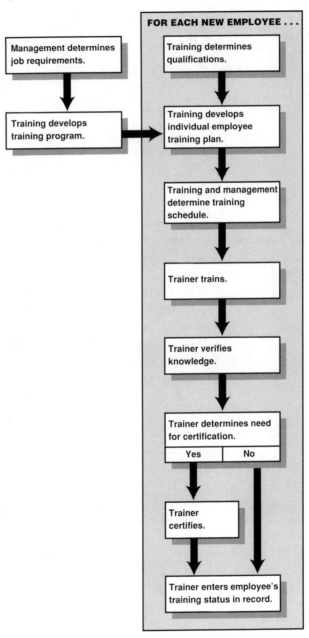

Continued on next page

**Required
documents and
records**

This table shows the information required in your controlled documents and quality records for this section of the Standard.

FOR . . .	INCLUDE information on . . .
controlled documents	• quality system training needs identification, • training process and procedures, • training modules, and • list of qualified trainers.
quality records	• personnel qualifications, • individual training plans, and • individual training results and necessary certifications.

Auditor questions

These are typical questions an auditor might ask for this section of the Standard.

- What is the training process?
- How are personnel who perform specific tasks qualified to do so on the basis of education, training, and experience?
- How are individual training schedules developed?
- How are results of training verified by testing or examination of personnel?
- Where necessary, how are personnel certified for specific tasks?
- How are records of training maintained?

4.19 Servicing

Requirement

When servicing is a specified requirement in the contract, your organization shall control that servicing and verify that it meets specified requirements.

What this means

Servicing is the after-sale attention provided by you on your product, frequently at the customer's site.

Example: An example of servicing is the maintenance service provided at the customer site on office copiers manufactured by your company.

What sections may apply

Servicing is an extension of your quality system and all of the sections of the Standard may apply. In particular, consider

- management, review, and auditing of personnel, often over wide areas;
- control of service manuals;
- training and possible need for certification of service personnel;
- supply of service parts;
- calibration of measuring and test equipment used in servicing;
- product and service nonconformance and corrective action; and
- service records.

Required documents and records

This table shows the information required in your controlled documents and quality records for this section of the Standard.

FOR . . .	INCLUDE information on . . .
controlled documents	• servicing requirements, • servicing processes and procedures, • training of servicing personnel, • calibration of any measuring equipment used for servicing, and • verification methods.

Continued on next page

4.19 Servicing, Continued

Required documents and records
(continued)

FOR ...	INCLUDE information on ...
quality records	• verification results, • calibration results on any measuring equipment, and • personnel training results and certifications as necessary.

Auditor questions

These are typical questions an auditor might ask for this section of the Standard.

- How are servicing requirements determined?
- What are the servicing processes?
- What are the procedures for performing and verifying service requirements specified in the contract?

4.20 Statistical Techniques

Requirement   **Your organization shall identify and use appropriate statistical techniques as necessary to verify the acceptability of process capability, product characteristics, and service.**

What this means   This means you need to

- have a process for identifying any necessary statistical techniques, and
- use any statistical techniques you identify as necessary in your quality system.

Note: A disclaimer that your quality system does not need statistical techniques probably will not suffice if the auditor observes a condition where acceptability of process capability, product characteristics, and service can be protected only by statistical techniques.

Using statistical techniques   Depending on your process and product complexity, the probability of needing statistical techniques for your quality system is highest in these sections of the Standard:

4.4   Design Control

4.9   Process Control

4.10   Inspection and Testing

4.11   Control of Inspection, Measuring, and Test Equipment

4.13   Control of Nonconforming Product, and

4.14   Corrective and Preventive Action.

Continued on next page

Required documents and records

This table shows the information required in your controlled documents and quality records for this section of the Standard.

FOR . . .	INCLUDE information on . . .
controlled documents	• process for determining need for statistical techniques, and • needed statistical techniques.
quality records	statistical results.

Auditor questions

These are typical questions an auditor might ask for this section of the Standard.

- What is the process for determining when statistical techniques are needed?
- What statistical techniques have been identified and used?
- How do you ensure that these techniques are used properly?
- How are test results of statistical techniques used?

Chapter 3

Strategic Planning

Overview

Introduction

This chapter focuses on the first stage of the certification process, strategic planning. Stage 1 sets the foundation for the certification effort, so proper planning is essential.

When this stage occurs

This timeline illustrates when strategic planning occurs.

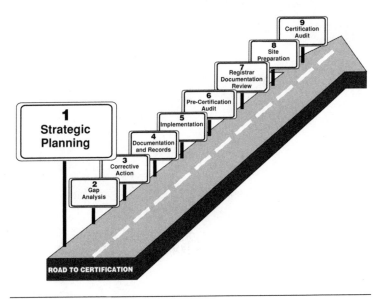

Continued on next page

Overview, Continued

In this chapter   This chapter contains the following topics:

Topic	See Page
Management Responsibilities	71
Selecting a Registrar	73
Selecting a Conformance Model	75
Forming a Project Team	77
Establishing a Timeline	80
Assessing the Organization's Training Needs	82

Management Responsibilities

Introduction	For the ISO certification process, management's responsibilities include the following:

- defining responsibility and authority,
- providing hands-on management of the project,
- assigning a full-time project leader,
- assigning project team members,
- providing adequate resources to get the job done,
- reviewing the quality system,
- providing adequate training to all personnel, and
- establishing a timeline without other projects taking priority.

Management commitment	Management commitment is a requirement for ensuring success of the certification process. Few projects succeed when there is no dedicated leader who ensures that the organization knows there is long-term management commitment.
	It is recommended that management take part as corrective action team members and writers of the documentation. This allows management visibly to show commitment as well as take part in achieving certification.

Assigning a project leader	Management should assign a project leader with direct access to management. This sends the message that management is committed to getting the organization's quality system certified.

Assigning a project team	Management should assign the project team according to the needs of the organization. A smaller or less complex organization may have a certification project core team of only three or four people. A larger or more complex organization may have a core team of a dozen or more people.
	Management should ensure that responsibility and authority for the certification project team is well defined. This is important due to

Continued on next page

Assigning a project team (continued)	• possible conflicts of interest—you may have multiple teams working on different projects. They may be interacting with each other and with other personnel working within the quality system; and
	• possible conflicts of responsibilities—team members will have other responsibilities that may compete for their limited time.
Providing adequate resources	Management should ensure that the project leader is provided with adequate resources to complete the project. The project team may need additional support, such as outside consulting, subject matter experts, technical experts, technical writers, or word-processing support. It is important that management responds to the project team's justified need for additional personnel.
Establishing a timeline	Management should set up a detailed timeline with milestones and responsibilities. All employees should be aware of this timeline, their role (*every* employee should have one), and exactly when they are responsible for completing their assigned task.
	This timeline keeps management and the employees focused on the goal and how it will be reached.
Providing adequate training	Management should ensure that the training needs of the organization are assessed and that training is provided according to those needs. Types of training to consider are

• comprehensive ISO 9000 orientation for the project team,
• familiarization with ISO 9000 for other members of the organization,
• documentation skills for those doing the writing or editing,
• ISO internal auditing for internal auditors, and
• quality system responsibilities for employees within the ISO certification process.

Selecting a Registrar

Introduction

The selection of a registrar should be completed as soon as possible in the strategic planning stage of the certification process.

What to look for

There are several areas management should investigate when selecting a registrar. Some questions to ask are:

- Is the registrar accepted in the countries in which you do business?
- Is the registrar knowledgeable about your industry and product/service?
- Does the registrar work with companies of differing sizes?
- Is the registrar accredited by an authorized (certified) body?
- Is the registrar financially secure? If not, what could happen if it goes bankrupt during or after your certification?
- Does the registrar maintain confidentiality agreements with its clients?
- What fees/actions occur if the certification process is suspended or cancelled?
- Is a specific registrar required by your customer?

Written information you should obtain

There are certain pieces of information that you should obtain from any registrar that you are considering using for your certification process. This information includes:

- references from other companies that have used the registrar,
- qualifications of the team that will be doing the auditing of your organization, and
- all costs involved with their process of certifying an organization, including exceptions.

Continued on next page

Cost

Always ask the registrar about the specific costs involved with certifying an organization for an ISO Standard and ongoing audits. Questions may include, but are not limited to, the following:

- How does the number of locations seeking certification affect the cost?
- How does the size of the organization affect the certification costs?
- What is the cost for the specific conformance model for which you are seeking certification (9001, 9002, or 9003)?
- How does the location of the organization versus the registrar affect the cost? Is there a local registrar that is accredited?
- How does the number of products/services seeking certification affect the cost?
- What fees are involved, especially after certification is attained and follow-up audits are required?

Selecting a Conformance Model

Introduction   Management, with the assistance of the selected registrar, should select a conformance model that is appropriate for the organization.

Guidelines for selection   The table provides guidelines for selecting a conformance model for your organization.

IF your organization . . .	THEN consider . . .
has significant product/service design activities,	9001.
manufactures products or delivers services according to • approved design, or • customer specifications. *Note*: This may be the case of companies without significant new product/service design activities.	9002.
has a product/service where the quality of this product/service is solely dependent on final inspection and testing. *Note*: This may be the case of distributors of certain products.	9003.

Important: If you have a customer or a regulatory agency that requires a specific ISO conformance model, then you must select that conformance model for the certification process.

Continued on next page

Selecting a Conformance Model, Continued

Selection process   This table provides the stages to be completed when selecting a conformance model that is appropriate for your organization.

Stage	Description
1	Read ISO 9000 to compare coverage of the three conformance models.
2	Select the appropriate conformance model (ISO 9001, 9002, or 9003).
3	Read the selected conformance model for requirements.
4	Read ISO 9004 • to confirm your choice of conformance model, and • for additional help in developing your quality system.
5	Consult with your registrar to verify your choice of conformance model.

Forming a Project Team

Introduction   The project team should be structured in such a way that all responsibilities and authority are understood by all in the organization.

Even though the project team is responsible for the certification process, all personnel within the organization should be given some responsibility so that the process succeeds.

Project team structure   This diagram is one approach to structuring your project team.

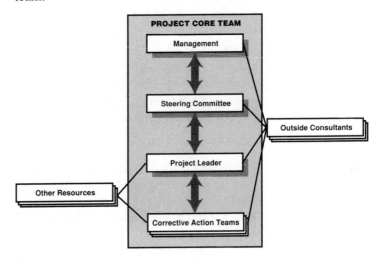

The project team members are discussed on the following pages.

Management   Management are responsible for providing the overall commitment and support to their organization to achieve ISO certification.

Continued on next page

Forming a Project Team, Continued

Steering committee

The steering committee is usually composed of the

- organization manager,
- organization mid-managers,
- representatives of key service organizations, and
- project leader for the certification project.

The steering committee's main responsibilities are

- providing input from each of the major areas of the organization,
- reviewing the status of the project,
- settling disputes,
- making decisions,
- demonstrating to the rest of the organization their strong commitment to this project, and
- assigning resources for the completion of the management requirements of the selected conformance model.

Project leader

The project leader should have access to management and a thorough knowledge of ISO 9000. Some organizations assign their ISO 9000 management representative as the project leader. The project leader's main responsibilities are

- providing tactical leadership for the project;
- assisting corrective action teams in attaining their goals;
- identifying, obtaining, and assigning other resources as necessary;
- serving as the interface with outside consultants; and
- providing the steering committee with timely status reports.

Corrective action teams

Corrective action teams concentrate their efforts on gap analysis, closure of identified gaps, and documenting any changes within the quality system. Generally, a corrective action team has three to five people knowledgeable on the subject of the section or sections of the Standard that they have been assigned.

Continued on next page

Additional resources

Although corrective action teams can take care of most of the gap analysis, there may be a need for additional resources in some instances. These resources may include

- other subject matter experts within the organization,
- technical editors or writers, and
- graphic artists, and so on.

Outside consulting

Your organization may want to enlist the help of outside consultants during the certification process. Areas where outside consultants appear to offer your greatest payback are:

- project strategizing and development;
- training in
  - ISO 9000,
  - internal audits for ISO 9000, and
  - documentation skills;
- corrective strategy development; and
- pre-assessment at the beginning of the process and readiness auditing shortly before the certification audit.

Treat outside consultants as one of your resources. Use them where they can do the job better than your internal resources, but do not totally rely on them as "an easy way out."

Establishing a Timeline

Introduction

Management should distribute two timelines:

- one that provides enough information to guide employees, and
- one that details the specifics of the project to guide management, the steering committee, and the project leader.

Importance of timeline

The timeline is an important communication tool. By keeping employees informed of changes/goals reached, you are including them in the certification process.

What to include

The certification process timeline used by management should include:

- milestones,
- a prepared budget,
- scheduled resources, and
- contingency plans.

The timeline should be used as a project management tool. If you currently have software that you use for project management, it will probably apply to the certification process as well.

Maintaining the timeline

The timeline should be updated as needed. Milestones should be highlighted when they are met.

After Gap Analysis

It is important for management to revisit the timeline once the gap analysis has been completed. At this time, critical phases may need to be modified.

Distribution

Both general (for organization) and specific (for project team) timelines should be distributed once revisions are made to them.

Continued on next page

Establishing a Timeline, Continued

Example: generic timeline

This is an example of a generic timeline that could be presented to employees.

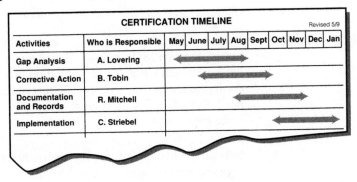

CERTIFICATION TIMELINE											Revised 5/9
Activities	**Who is Responsible**	May	June	July	Aug	Sept	Oct	Nov	Dec	Jan
Gap Analysis	A. Lovering	◄═══════►								
Corrective Action	B. Tobin			◄═══════►						
Documentation and Records	R. Mitchell					◄═══════►				
Implementation	C. Striebel							◄═══════►		

Assessing the Organization's Training Needs

Introduction   Management is responsible for having the organization's training needs assessed.

ISO training   It is important that management and your organization receive the appropriate ISO training. Management may need a higher-level approach to the ISO certification process and the selected conformance model, whereas the rest of the organization may need more detailed information about ISO or documentation since they will be working within the quality system every day.

Selecting a handful of employees to attend ISO auditor training may help provide a more thorough gap analysis.

Organization training   It is recommended that some training, formal or informal, be provided to your organization so that everyone is working from the same model and the following are understood:

- purpose of the organization,
- limits of the quality system,
- products/services and their purchasers,
- incoming materials and their suppliers,
- product flow through the quality system process,
- process and product/service measurement needs,
- responsibilities,
- key supporting organizations and their responsibilities, and
- existing documents and their records.

Chapter 4

Gap Analysis and Corrective Action

Overview

Introduction

This chapter describes

- gap analysis,
- corrective action,
- corrective action teams, and
- the gap analysis and corrective action process.

When these stages occur

This diagram illustrates when gap analysis and corrective action occur.

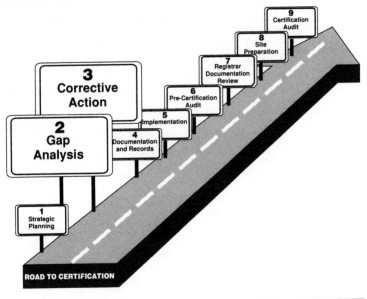

Continued on next page

Overview, Continued

In this chapter   This chapter contains the following topics:

Descriptions of Gap Analysis and Corrective Action

Gap analysis

Gap analysis is the comparison of an existing quality system to one or more sets of external requirements. This analysis determines if there are any gaps between the two.

The primary set of external requirements is the ISO 9000 conformance model (ISO 9001, 9002, or 9003) selected by your organization. Other sets of external requirements may be statutory or regulatory.

Example: The Federal Food and Drug Administration's *Good Manufacturing Practices* for medical device products is an example of a regulatory set of requirements.

Other Possible Gaps. The corrective action team should also ensure during gap analysis that there are no gaps between

- existing documents and actual quality system operations, and
- existing document record requirements and actual records.

Corrective action

Corrective action is the closure of gaps between the existing quality system and what is required in the external set of requirements.

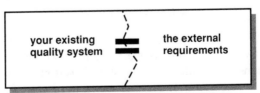

The corrective action team should also close any gaps between existing documents and actual quality system operations, and between existing documents record requirements and actual records.

Corrective Action Teams

Description

A *corrective action team* is a project team of personnel formed for the purpose of performing both the gap analysis and the corrective action. The gap analysis and corrective action may be performed for one or more functions of the set of external requirements.

Corrective action team assignment

An individual corrective action team would do the gap analysis and corrective action on one or more sections of the selected ISO 9000 conformance model.

The project leader should ensure that all the sections of the selected conformance model are covered by corrective action teams.

Example team assignment

This might be one approach to corrective action team section assignments.

Management Corrective Action Team	Documentation Corrective Action Team	Purchasing Corrective Action Team	Process Corrective Action Team	Product Corrective Action Team
• management responsibility • contract review • corrective and preventive action • internal audits • training	• quality system • document and data control • control of quality records	• purchasing • control of customer-supplied product	• process control • control of inspection equipment • handling, storage, preservation, packaging, and delivery • servicing • statistical techniques	• design control • product identification and traceability • inspection and testing • test status • nonconforming product

Makeup of corrective action teams

Corrective action teams usually are composed of personnel from your organization who have subject matter expertise on the quality system function(s) being analyzed and the comparable sections of the conformance model. As appropriate, you may have personnel from supporting organizations, subcontractors, or even customers.

Gap Analysis and Corrective Action Process

Process

This table shows the stages of the gap analysis and corrective action process.

Note: The corrective action team is doing this process for each specific quality system function and/or the comparable section of the conformance model.

Stage	What the Corrective Action Team Does
1	• Identifies the requirements of the selected conformance model (ISO 9001, 9002, or 9003); and • identifies any corporate, regulatory, or statutory requirements.

2	• Resolves any differences between the requirements of the conformance model and any applicable
	  • regulatory requirements,
	  • statutory requirements, and
	  • corporate requirements.

3	Identifies the existing process in the quality system. *Note*: There may not be an existing process.
4	• Identifies the existing process supporting documents, • compares documents to the existing process, and • resolves conflicts between process and documents.
5	Compares the existing quality system to the external requirements to identify any gaps.
6	Develops any necessary changes to existing process to close the gaps and obtains approval from management.
7	Develops new documents or changes existing documents as necessary and obtains approval from management. *Note*: See Chapters 5 and 6 for additional detail on document development.
8	Assists management in training of personnel and implementation of changes.
9	• Verifies effectiveness of any changes over time, and • repeats Stages 5 through 8 as necessary to correct ineffective changes.

Stage 1: Requirements Identification

What happens

During Stage 1, the corrective action team determines the requirements for those functions for which it is responsible in the various external requirements.

Maintaining a master list

It is probably best at this time to maintain a master list of the requirements for each function and the source of each requirement. This will ensure that a requirement is not lost and will help later in identifying conflicting requirements.

Example of requirements

This table shows external requirements to consider and gives examples.

IF an external requirement is ...	THEN an example may be ...
an ISO 9000 Conformance Model,	ISO 9002.
other ISO or ANSI Standards,	ISO 10011.
regulatory or statutory,	• Atomic Energy Commission, • Food and Drug Administration (FDA), • military standards (MIL-STD), or • Postal regulations.
an industrial association agreements or guidelines,	• American Society for Testing and Materials (ASTM), or • Society of Automotive Engineers (SAE).
corporate policies, rules, processes, or methods,	• records management policy, • no smoking rule, • safety glasses rule, or • document numbering.

Stage 2: Resolution of Requirements Differences

What happens   During Stage 2, the corrective action team resolves inconsistencies between conflicting external requirements.

Conflicting requirement sources   Where there is a direct conflict between two requirement sources, the team needs to resolve the conflict. This may require

- conforming to the stricter requirement,
- conforming to both requirements, or
- resolving the conflict.

Note: The requirements from the two external sources may contradict each other, so it may be necessary to work with the two sources to resolve the conflict.

Result of this stage   The team should end this stage with a complete list of all requirements and the external source(s) for each.

Requirements	External Sources
1. _____	1. _____
2. _____	2. _____
3. _____	3. _____

Stage 3: Existing Process Evaluation

What happens During Stage 3, the corrective action team identifies the existing process.

Example process elements This table shows typical elements of the process to be identified and an example of its application to the control of quality records.

Element of Process	Application to Control of Quality Records
Purpose	Retain records for quality and legal reasons.
Limits	Only quality records included in the process.
Product(s) and customer	Product: master copy of record; customer: management.
Incoming material(s) and subcontractor	Incoming material: record data; subcontractor: data recorder.
Product flow	Path of individual record from initiation through filing and storage to disposition.
Process and product measurement needs	Storage volume needs.
Responsibilities of personnel	Responsibilities of recorder, filer, and master copy holder.
Key supporting organizations and their responsibilities	Key supporting organization: Corporate Records Management; responsibility: long-term storage of records.

Stage 4: Existing Document Compatibility

What happens

During Stage 4, the corrective action team

- identifies all existing documents supporting that process,
- compares existing documents to the present process, and
- resolves any conflicts between processes and documents.

Identification of documents

This should include identification of controlled documents, records, notes on the wall, electronic mail messages, equipment manuals, engineering drawings, practical standards, or other tangible means of information transfer.

Comparison to present process

Comparing the present process to the documents should include interviewing supervisors and operators, and observing the process to ensure that there are no gaps between documents and actual operation of the process.

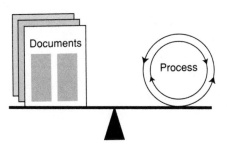

Note: If Stage 3 has been done effectively, the comparison effort should be minimized.

Resolution of conflicts

The purpose of the resolution is to establish a baseline for the team, using either the documents or the actual operation of the process where conflict is apparent. The team should not spend an excessive amount of time rewriting documents to match the way the process is being done, as everything may change after the gap analysis.

Warning

This stage is an important foundation for future stages. Failure of the team to understand fully the existing process will probably result in a revisiting of this stage and lost time.

Stage 5: Gap Analysis

What happens   During Stage 5, the corrective action team compares the existing process to the primary external requirement for each element of the requirement.

Diagram   This is a diagram of the comparison of the quality system process to the external requirements.

the existing process
(from Stages 3 & 4)

the GAP

primary external requirement
(from Stages 1 & 2)

Result of this stage   A list of each element of the requirement should be maintained showing conformance or nonconformance and the nature of each nonconformance.

Stage 6: Process Corrective Action

What happens

During Stage 6, the corrective action team evaluates each non-conformance and develops a change or modification that will bring the process into conformance.

Note: Where no existing process exists, this will mean the development of the entire process.

Example

Before: The corrective action team for documentation finds that there is no identified document control process. Everyone in the quality system initiates documents as they see fit and document authorization is nonexistent.

After: The team develops a policy, process, and procedures for document control. These will serve later as the basis for the documents for document and data control.

Note: As for any development, changes to the quality system need to be approved by the appropriate authority.

Stage 7: Document Corrective Action

What happens   During Stage 7, the corrective action team

- determines what documents are needed,
- develops the identified documents,
- verifies the documents through review,
- validates the documents through a practical trial with personnel who will use them, and
- obtains authorization for publication.

Note: See Chapter 5 for additional details on this stage.

Result
of this stage   The results of this stage are new and revised documents, as well as the disposition of obsolete documents.

Stage 8: Training and Implementation

What happens   During Stage 8, the corrective action team

- assists training personnel and management to train those personnel affected by any changes, and
- assists management in the coordination of the change implementation.

Training   Training may include

- explanation,
- demonstration,
- a review of the documents, and
- practical hands-on operation of the process.

Implementation   Changes should be implemented at a set time, to ensure that all personnel are aware that the change has taken place. Management should take an active role in ensuring that the change is effective during the implementation.

At this time, the risk of something going wrong is high. Even trained personnel may still be unfamiliar with the new way of performing their jobs. Therefore hands-on management will be necessary until the transition from old to new is complete.

Stage 9: Change Effectiveness Verification

What happens
During Stage 9 the corrective action team assists management in verifying that the change is effective.

Time to complete
This stage may take up to three months to complete.

Result of this stage
At the end of this stage, there should be a complete turnover of all responsibility for the change from the corrective action team and project leadership to the process management.

Chapter 5

Implementing a Document Structure

Overview

Introduction   It is important to develop a consistent structure for your documents, since a visible structure and document trail are required by most auditors.

This chapter provides an approach to structuring your documents.

When this occurs   This timeline illustrates when a document structure should be developed.

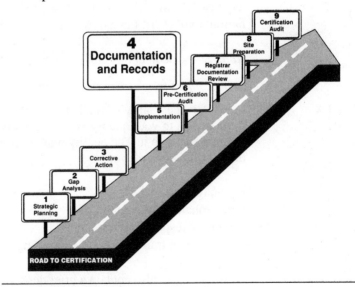

In this chapter   This chapter contains the following topics:

Topic	See Page
ISO Document Levels	98
Organizing your Documents	100
Creating a Functional Breakdown of your Documents	102

ISO Document Levels

Introduction

The ISO Standard provides a typical quality system *document hierarchy*, sometimes called the *documentation pyramid*.

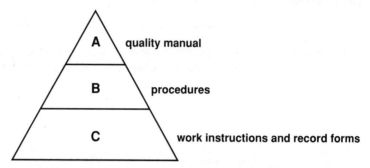

The document hierarchy is in the form of a pyramid because there is only one document at the top level, supported by an increasing number of documents as you proceed through the bottom two levels. Each of the three levels is described below.

Note: Some people may call the three levels "1, 2, and 3."

Level A

Level A is the quality manual. This serves as a documented introduction to your quality system, usually to a reader who is not familiar with it. The quality manual contains, for each section of the Standard, your

- management policy,
- a rationale for the policy,
- primary responsibilities, and
- a document trail to Level B supporting documents.

It probably will also contain a brief description of your organization, its primary process, and its major products or services.

A quality manual is usually not very large. A typical quality manual might be 20 to 30 pages.

Continued on next page

Level B

Level B describes what happens. It contains documents, identified in the Standard as procedures, describing each process in your quality system.

A typical Level B document might contain

- definitions of terms used in the process description,
- a description of the process,
- process responsibilities, and
- a document trail to Level C documents in support of the process.

Level C

Level C tells how to do something. It contains documents, identified in the Standard as *work instructions*, telling the reader how to carry out specific operations or tasks.

Note: Many organizations in the United States identify documents in Level C with terms such as *standard operating procedures*, *test methods*, *operating instructions*, or just *procedures*. You should ensure that your corrective action team members understand that the use of the term *procedure* in the Standard generally applies to the requirement for documents describing a process.

A typical Level C document might contain

- reference data such as specifications, standards, or product lists;
- training for specific operations;
- hands-on directions such as instructions or checklists;
- formats for forms; and
- a document trail to any other supporting documents, usually in Level C.

Organizing your Documents

Introduction

To begin organizing your documents, project teams should meet to create an organizational chart of all documents within the quality system. This may take some time, but it is necessary to identify which documents are part of the quality system (including federal, state, and other regulatory documents) and which are not.

Benefits to organizing

Organizing your documents also provides

- another means to analyzing your quality system and seeing where gaps may be occurring, and
- a hierarchy from which you can begin thinking about a document numbering system.

Example

This chart provides an example of how to organize your documents by levels.

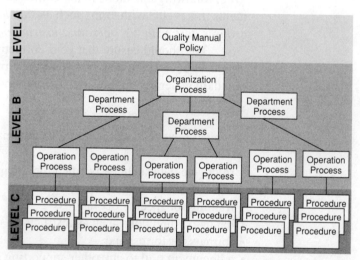

Job Aid. Some organizations have found it helpful to put the names of individual documents on little yellow "stickies" and then post them on available wall space. This allows you to move documents from one location in the structure to another.

Continued on next page

Organizing your Documents, Continued

Non–quality system documents

While you are charting your quality system documents, it is important to keep a list of those documents that are *not* part of your quality system. If documents do not have an impact on the quality of your product/service, then they do not have to be a part of the quality system documentation.

Examples of non–quality system documents may be:

Important: You must identify non–quality system documents if you choose to have a single document control process covering all of your documents.

Documents from other organizations

If documents from other organizations do have an impact on the quality of your organization's product, then you are required to include or reference them in your quality system documentation. These documents may be:

• operator or troubleshooting manuals for equipment,
• software operating manuals, or
• regulatory test methods.

Recommendation: Incorporate these documents (or extracts or portions of these documents) into your quality system controlled document structure, and indicate that your organization will provide copy control, but not content control.

Creating a Functional Breakdown
of your Documents

Introduction

Once you have created an organizational chart of your documents, you can further break them down by function (or department, division, etc.). By structuring your documents by function, it is easier

- to determine which sections to assign to corrective action teams for gap analysis, and
- to control your documents.

An example approach follows.

Functional approach

To break down your documents by function, first look at the conformance model that your organization has selected to identify what sections must be covered. Then group the sections into functions that are appropriate for your organization.

You may decide that five to seven groupings may be sufficient for forming corrective action teams or controlling the documentation.

Example

This diagram shows one approach to grouping sections of ISO Standard 9001.

Management	Process

4.1 management responsibility
4.3 contract review
4.14 corrective and preventive
      action
4.17 internal quality audits
4.18 training
	4.9 process control
	4.11 control of inspection,
	      measuring, and test
	      equipment
	4.15 handling, storage,
	      packaging, preservation,
	      and delivery
	4.20 statistical techniques

Documentation	**Product**
4.2 quality system 4.5 document and data control	4.4 design control 4.8 product identification and traceability

Continued on next page

Creating a Functional Breakdown
of your Documents, Continued

Example
(continued)

Documentation	Product
4.16 control of quality records	4.10 inspection and testing 4.12 inspection and test status 4.13 control of nonconforming product
Purchasing	**Service**
4.6 purchasing 4.7 control of customer- supplied product	4.19 servicing

Advantages

The advantages of grouping the sections functionally are that

- project team members know what they are responsible for and have a clearer focus of the scope of their tasks during gap analysis, corrective action, writing documentation, and implementation; and

- document control team members have logical document "chunks" that will be easier to assign and control.

Next step

From the breakdown of documents, your document coordination and corrective action teams can begin

- developing a Table of Contents,
- developing templates, and
- interviewing workers and observing the quality system to correct the gaps.

Chapter 6

Document Development

Overview

Introduction   This chapter provides guidelines for the document development process.

When this occurs   This timeline illustrates when the document development process occurs.

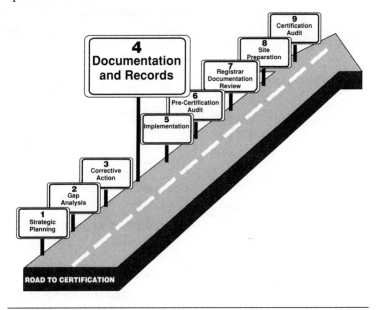

In this chapter   This chapter contains the following topics:

The Document Development Process

The document development process may be used for

- creating documents, or
- revising documents.

Process

This table shows a typical document development process.

Stage	Description
1	Somebody sees need for new or revised document and submits change request to document coordinator.
	When ... / **Then ...**
	a new document is required, → the document coordinator assigns a document owner and authorizer.
	a revision to existing document is required, → the document coordinator forwards the change to document owner.
2	Document owner completes document preliminary planning.
3	Document owner completes initial draft, reviews it with fellow subject matter experts, makes any necessary changes, and forwards content-revised draft on to document coordinator.
4	Document coordinator reviews content-revised draft, prepares final draft for publication, and forwards final draft to document authorizer.
5	**When the authorizer ...** / **Then the authorizer ...**
	feels content is satisfactory, → signs approval for publication and returns final draft to document coordinator.
	has questions or recommendations for content improvement, → resolves these with document owner prior to signing approval for publication.

Continued on next page

Process,
(continued)

Stage	Description
6	Document coordinator prepares necessary copies and distributes to individual copy owners as necessary.
7	Individual copy owners ensure • changes are reviewed with those concerned, • necessary training is completed, • document is implemented as scheduled, and • any older copies are discarded as necessary.

Stages of the Document Development Process

Introduction	This is a review of each of the seven stages of the document development process.

Stage 1: **need recognition**	Anyone, inside or outside your organization, may initiate a document revision or identify a document need due to changes in the quality system. Your document coordinator probably is your best focal point for these change recommendations. Working within guidelines from management, the document coordinator can assign a *document owner*, *document authorizer*, and a *document identification number (DIN)* for new documents. *Note*: It is recommended that every document in your quality system have an individual document owner responsible for its content. This document owner should be a subject matter expert on the document content.

Stage 2: **preliminary** **planning**	The document owner assesses the document to be written or revised. This assessment includes: • who is the audience? • what is the purpose of the document? • what resources are available (available data, subject matter experts, technical writers)? and • where are there gaps in the available data?

Stage 3: **initial draft**	The document owner writes the initial draft of the documentation. Other subject matter experts and a technical writer may provide assistance as necessary. The document owner should select a review team of subject matter experts and also potential readers of the document. This can be relatively informal, with rewrites until everyone is satisfied.

Continued on next page

Stages of the Document Development
Process, Continued

Stage 3: **initial draft,** (continued)	The document owner should forward the completed content-revised draft on to the document coordinator, with a proposed list for approved-copy distribution. *Note*: The draft may or may not be properly formatted at this point, depending on the documenting skills of the document owner.
Stage 4: **final draft**	The document coordinator ensures that the final draft of the document meets all guidelines. This might include • spell checking, • grammar, • format, • page numbering, • appropriate title, and • DIN and effective date of implementation. The document coordinator then forwards the final draft to the assigned authorizer, with a cover sheet known as a *Document Change Notice (DCN)*. *Note*: We recommend that there be only one authorizer for each document, and that the authorizer be a subject matter expert no more than one level above the document owner.
Stage 5: **authorization**	The authorizer reviews the document prior to distribution. When the authorizer has questions about the content or has recommendations on how to improve it, these are discussed directly with the document owner rather than by going back through the document coordinator. When necessary, the final draft may be returned to the document owner for additional rework. Stages 3 through 5 would then be repeated until the final draft is acceptable to the authorizer. The authorizer then signs the *Document Change Notice* approving publication of the document. Both the DCN and the final draft are returned to the document coordinator.

Continued on next page

Stages of the Document Development Process, Continued

Stage 6:
distribution

The document coordinator

- distributes copies of the document to designated copy holders,
- retains the signed copy of the DCN and the document,
- updates the *Document Master List* to reflect change, and
- retains a copy of any superseded document, clearly marked as such, as a record of change.

Stage 7:
individual copy

The holders of individual copies are responsible for ensuring that

- all concerned personnel are aware of content changes,
- any necessary training is completed,
- the document is implemented on the effective date, and
- copies of superseded documents are discarded.

Note: Management ensures proper control of individual copies by assigning copy holder responsibilities. When a copy holder is transferred, a new copy holder should be assigned as part of the transfer process.

Change Notification

How to do it

The Standard requires that all appropriate parties be notified of any document changes. The following are ways to accomplish this:

- The change may be highlighted in some manner on the document,
- key points of the change may be included in a topic titled "change" on the document, or
- a document change notice may be attached to the document copy for distribution.

Sample Document Change Notice

This is an example of a *Document Change Notice*.

DATE: 8/15/94
TO: Users of document 4.4.313
FROM: Document Control
SUBJECT: CHANGE NOTIFICATION

Purpose This memo serves as a change notification for document 4.4.313 "Work Instruction/Customer Supplied Product Document Check."

Location of change The change is found on page 5 in steps 3 and 4 of the work instruction.

Change The changes are described in the table below.

Current	Revised
Step 3: Complete Form 15B.	Step 3: Complete Form 11.
Step 4: Send completed Form 15B to the purchasing agent listed on the bottom left of the shipping form.	Step 4: Send completed Form 11 to the Quality Assurance Department.

Action Immediately make note of changes in your current documentation. You will receive a revised copy of document 4.4.313 on 9/15/94. Upon receipt of the revised document, dispose of the out-of-date document and replace with the revised document.

111

Chapter 7

Instituting Document and Quality Record Controls

Overview

Introduction

This chapter describes controls for documents and records. There are different control measures because documents and records are *not* the same.

- A *document* describes how the quality system operates (what happens, how to do it, etc.).
- A *record* provides objective evidence that the quality system operates according to the document.

Control of documents

To maintain control of your quality system documents, your organization should

- develop a formal document structure;
- assign ownership of each document to one person;
- develop, distribute, and maintain writing guidelines;
- assign Document Identification Numbers (DINs) to all documents; and
- maintain a master list of all documents and issue it periodically.

Note: Developing a document structure is covered in Chapter 5.

Control of quality records

A control of quality records process should be in place to maintain all quality records.

When this occurs

This timeline illustrates when document controls should be instituted.

Continued on next page

Overview, Continued

When this occurs,
(continued)

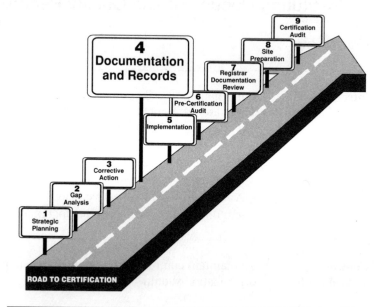

In this chapter

This chapter contains the following topics:

Topic	See Page
Assigning Document Responsibilities	115
Instituting Writing Guidelines	117
Implementing Document Identification Numbers	118
Maintaining a Master List	120
Control of Quality Records Process	123
Stages of the Control of Quality Records Process	124

Assigning Document Responsibilities

Introduction   Assigning document responsibilities is a document control measure that involves

- document owners,
- copy owners,
- document authorizers, and
- the document coordinator.

Document responsibilities are provided below.

Document owner   The content of individual documents is the responsibility of the *document owner* (someone with expertise in the subject matter). That document owner usually enlists the help of other subject matter experts to act first as input resources and later as the document content review team.

One document owner should be responsible for the content of a particular document. A document should never be assigned to an entire department or the document coordinator. This ensures accountability for maintenance of the document.

Copy ownership   *Copy owners* are those who maintain individual copies of controlled documents. They have several responsibilities, including

- ensuring security of documents from tampering or theft,
- not writing on the documents,
- ensuring availability of a current version of the document, and
- discarding copies of superseded documents.

Document authorizer   The *authorizer* approves publication of a new document or changes to an existing document. The document authorizer ideally should be someone who has expertise in the subject matter contained within the document. Management should identify appropriate authorizers for each group and level of documents.

Continued on next page

Document coordinator

The *document coordinator* should

- develop, maintain, and distribute a document change process;
- develop, maintain, and distribute writing guidelines and templates;
- develop, maintain, and distribute the master list of all quality system documents;
- maintain all document change records;
- assist document owners as necessary in document writing;
- review completed documents for spelling, grammer, format, and document control entries; and
- routinely audit individual copies of documents to ensure that the most current version is being used and it is clean of notes or tampering.

Instituting Writing Guidelines

Introduction

The use of writing guidelines will allow relatively inexperienced writers at all levels of your organization to create documents that are recognizable and readable.

Who should receive the writing guidelines

Those who should receive a copy of the writing guidelines are

- the document coordinator,
- document owners,
- authorizers, and
- anyone else who needs them.

What to include in the writing guidelines

The writing guidelines might include

- templates for frequently used document types,
- formatting styles,
- common terms,
- use of file names,
- acceptable documenting software, and
- organization and sequence information.

Why writing guidelines are important

Guidelines lead to consistently styled documents that

- readers can recognize and be able to understand, and
- writers and reviewers can create and change quickly.

Online guidelines

If your quality system documentation is online, then you must also include detailed guidelines for online documentation. Guidelines should be listed for screen design, navigational design, when to use links, pop-up windows, graphics, and so on.

Implementing Document Identification Numbers

Introduction

One of the document controls implemented by the document control department is the use of Document Identification Numbers (DINs).

Purpose of DINs

The *Document Identification Number (DIN)* tracks documents and provides a visible hierarchy of the quality system documentation.

Who uses DINs

The document coordinator, employees, and auditors use these numbers for different reasons.

THE ...	USES the DIN to ...
document coordinator	track versions of documents.
employee	reference other documents.
auditor	ensure that the correct information is available to the employee who performs a job.

Example 1

This example is one approach to document identification numbering after using the organizational chart approach.

Continued on next page

Example 1,
(continued)

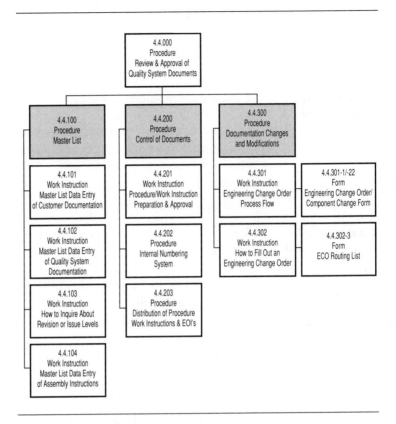

Example 2

This example is an approach to document identification numbering based on each section of the Standard selected by your organization.

4.13.315	
Number	**Description**
4.13	Indicates the section of the Standard; Control of Nonconforming Product.
3	Indicates that the document is a Level C document (or in numbers, a Level 3 document).
15	Indicates that this is the fifteenth procedure documented within this section and at this level.

Maintaining a Master List

Introduction

The document coordinator is responsible for maintaining a document master list or similar means of ensuring that personnel are aware of the current version of each document.

When to issue the master list

The master list should be issued

- on a scheduled basis (monthly, semi-annually, etc.),
- when document revisions occur frequently, or
- when the document coordination team sees a need for more frequent distribution.

What to include on the master list

A document master list or equivalent should include, at a minimum, the

- Document Identification Number (DIN),
- document name, and
- effective date of current version in distribution.

Note: Try to keep all the information for one document in a single-line entry.

Example 1: master list

Below is an example of a page from a master list.

Note: The document from page 119 is listed in this master list.

DOCUMENT MASTER LIST				
DIN	Document Name	Last Revision Date	Document Originator	Distribution List(s)
4.11.359	How to operate xyz machine	10/1/94	P. Flynn	Operators Managers Technicians
4.13.315	How to track maintenance calls	1/3/94	N. Hanson	Managers
4.15.261	Clearing filters	5/13/94	D. Elwood	Technicians

Continued on next page

Maintaining a Master List, Continued

How to organize

One approach to organizing the master list in a software application is to sequence it by document types (this may also be done for documents that are not part of the quality system as shown below).

Example:

- ISO
  - Level A
  - Level B
  - Level C
  - Masters
    - 4.1
    - 4.2
    - 4.3
    - **4.4 (see next page)**
- HR
- Facility
- IS

Continued on next page

Example 2:
master list

This is an example of a master list of all quality system documents for 4.4 Document Control.

Note: See page 119 to see the organizational chart used to create this master list.

Part Number	Part Description	Product Code
4.4.000	Proc, Review & Apprvl Qlty Sys Docs	6000
4.4.100	Proc, Master List	6000
4.4.101	WI, Mstr List Data Entry of Cstm Docs	6100
4.4.102	WI, Mstr List Data Entry of Int Docs	6100
4.4.103	WI, How to Inqre Revisions and Issues	6100
4.4.104	WI, Mstr List Data Entry of Assy Instr	6000
4.4.200	Proc, Control of Documents	6100
4.4.202	Proc, Internal Numbering System	6000
4.4.203	Proc, Distr of Procs, WI & EOI's	6000
4.4.300	Proc, Doc Changes and Modifications	6100
4.4.301	WI, Eng Change Order Process Flow	6000
4.4.301-1	Form, Engineering Change Order	6100
4.4.301-2	Form, Component Change Form	6000
4.4.302	WI, How to Fill Out an ECO	6300
4.4.302-3	Form, ECO Routing List	6300

Control of Quality Records Process

Introduction   Often the process for retaining records for legal reasons is not always sufficient for meeting the certification audit requirements of ISO 9000 quality systems.

A process for controlling quality records in order to meet the certification audit requirements is discussed below.

Process diagram   A typical control of quality records process is shown in this diagram.

1   RECORD   Record Need Identification

2   RECORD REQUIREMENTS   Collection Method Identification

3   Data Collection

4   Changes Batch Audit   Indexing

5   Filing

6   Storage

7   Disposition

Stages of the Control of Quality Records Process

Introduction

The seven requirements for controlling quality records called for in the ISO 9000 Standard are provided below.

Note: See the previous diagram for a graphic representation of the control of quality records process.

Stage 1: record need identification

In Stage 1, the following actions should be performed:

- define responsibilities,
- identify record need,
- determine the content of the record,
- set a retention schedule (usually based on importance and product/service life),
- retain individual copies,
- determine ownership of the record, and
- determine how form revisions will be handled.

Note: *Retention* is the amount of time a record should be saved before disposition.

Stage 2: collection method identification

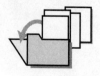

In Stage 2, the following actions should be performed:

- identify what is required for each record,
- indicate when collection for each record is done,
- determine how collection is recorded,
- determine whether reporting is required,
- maintain each record, and
- determine responsibilities for each task.

Stage 3: data collection

All records, as indicated from Stage 2, are collected.

Continued on next page

Stages of the Control of Quality Records
Process, Continued

Stage 4: indexing

Individual record copies are identified to ensure proper

- filing,
- storage,
- possible retrieval, and
- subsequent disposition.

Stage 5: filing

Individual record copies are placed in specific locations of storage.

Stage 6: storage

Adequate storage facilities are provided to minimize deterioration, damage, or loss. This stage is divided into two parts. They are:

- *On-site* storage. This ensures the availability of the records during the period when frequent retrieval may be necessary.

- *Centralized* storage. This provides a secure means of storage during the period when retrieval needs are rare but a requirement for retention exists. Centralized storage makes best use of limited on-site storage facilities.

Stage 7: disposition

Disposition of records means discarding at a predetermined time.

At the predetermined time for disposition, the record should be disposed by quality records control personnel without any requirement for authorization by the record owner. Records differ from controlled documents, as controlled documents are retained until they are revised or until discard is authorized.

Chapter 8

Site Preparation

Overview

Introduction   This chapter explains how to prepare your organization for the certification audit.

When this occurs   This timeline illustrates when certification preparation occurs.

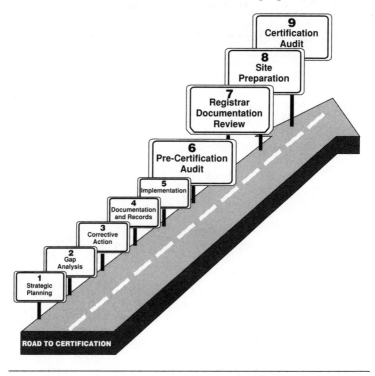

Continued on next page

Overview, Continued

The Pre-Certification Audit

Description	The pre-certification audit is an audit performed to ensure that your organization's quality system and documentation conform to the ISO 9000 Standard for which you are seeking certification.
When it happens	The pre-certification audit is done just prior to the official certification audit.
Who does it	Trained internal auditors, an outside consultant, the registrar, or a combination of the three may perform the pre-certification audit.
What happens	An audit is performed to assess the organization's quality system and documentation to ensure that all nonconformances from the gap analysis have been corrected and implemented according to the selected conformance model.
How long it takes	The pre-certification audit usually takes two days or more depending on the size, number of facilities, and complexity of your quality system.
Advantages	The advantages to performing a pre-certification audit are that • your organization gets practice answering auditor questions, • employees gain an understanding of what to expect from the auditors, and • employees may find previously overlooked nonconformances.

The Registrar Documentation Review

Introduction   The registrar uses your documentation to review your organization's quality system.

When it happens   The registrar reviews the documentation prior to the site visit for the certification audit.

What happens   The registrar reviews your organization's quality manual and any other documents that he or she wishes to review.

The registrar may review these documents at your organization's site, or he or she may review the documents at his or her offices. The latter saves money and time.

What the registrar is looking for   The registrar reviews the quality system documents to be sure that they have addressed all requirements of the ISO conformance model for which your organization is seeking certification.

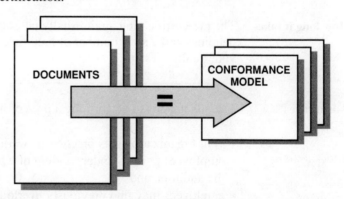

If the documents do *not* address all requirements of the ISO conformance model for which your organization is seeking certification, then the registrar may postpone the certification visit until your documents are corrected.

How long it takes   The registrar may take three days or more to review the documents.

Preparing Management
for the Certification Audit

Introduction
The management of your organization must be prepared for the certification auditors and ensure that employees are also prepared.

How to prepare
Management should prepare itself by

- being familiar with the quality manual and the quality system,
- taking advantage of the initial interview (if the registrar requests one) to get familiar with the registrar,
- walking through operations and performing spot-check audits,
- confirming that all nonconformances found in the pre-certification audit have been corrected, and
- confirming schedules and needs of the certification team.

Arranging for guides
The management committee must select responsible employees to act as "guides" for the certification auditors. It is important that the employees selected

- are knowledgeable of the quality system and how it operates,
- know when to step in and clarify other employees' answers to auditor questions, and
- are helpful and diplomatic, not overbearing, to the certification team.

Reserving office space
Certification auditors will need an office or conference room in which to meet and discuss findings. Be sure that office space is reserved prior to their visit and made available to them throughout their stay.

Also be sure that this office space has adequate office supplies and equipment (for example, a telephone) for the certification auditors. Confirming the audit team's needs prior to their arrival will save time and unneeded frustration.

Continued on next page

Preparing Management
for the Certification Audit, Continued

Restricted areas   It is important to allow auditors to view all areas within your quality system. However, there may be some rare cases when an area is restricted. If your organization has some areas that are restricted, then be sure to inform the certification auditors prior to their arrival at your site.

If you are allowing the certification auditors into areas that are normally restricted, then be sure that employees working in that area and security personnel are informed prior to the arrival of the certification auditors.

Preparing your Organization for the Certification Audit

Introduction   Your organization will have concerns and uncertainties about what happens during the audit and what they are supposed to do.

How to prepare   Preparing your organization for the certification audit can be done in a number of ways, such as

- holding formal training sessions,
- distributing booklets or manuals about the certification audit,
- performing internal audits,
- sending e-mails with daily or weekly tips,
- distributing online documentation, and/or
- hanging posters with tips.

Information to include   Employees should be prepared for the certification audit with information such as

- the objectives and scope of the audit,
- the need to be *honest* and cooperative,
- the fact that the audit is not a review of job performance, it is a review of the *system*,
- the need to have all documents that are pertaining to his or her job within the quality system available, and
- guidelines for how to answer auditor questions.

Answering auditor questions   Employees should be provided with tips or formal training on how to answer auditor questions. Tips to include are:

- do not be misleading or defensive when an auditor asks a question;
- do not answer a question with an answer that you think the registrar wants to hear;
- answer only the question; you do not need to volunteer more information than the answer requires;

Continued on next page

Preparing your Organization
for the Certification Audit, Continued

Answering auditor questions, (continued)

- do not try to answer a question if you do not know the answer, just say you do not know; and
- ask the registrar to clarify the question that he or she is asking you if you do not understand it.

After the audit

It is important to remind employees that once the audit is over and the registrar leaves, operations cannot go back to the way they were before this certification effort began.

Operations and documents should be maintained because follow-up (or surveillance) audits will be performed by internal and external auditors on a regular basis.

The Certification Audit

Introduction

Your organization is now ready to have the registrar perform the certification audit.

What happens

The registrar visits your site(s) to

- meet with the upper management to provide an overview of what will occur while they are there and answer any of management's questions, and

- determine whether or not your quality system is implemented according to the selected conformance model and the quality system documentation. To assess your quality system, the registrar asks your employees questions and observes employees performing their jobs.

What to expect

Follow the table below to see the possible outcomes of the certification audit.

IF your organization's quality system . . .	THEN the registrar . . .
conforms to the selected ISO 9000 Standard,	grants certification of your quality system.
has a minimal amount of nonconformances,	grants certification of your quality system. *Note*: Certification may be contingent upon correction of nonconformances.
has many nonconformances,	does *not* grant certification. *Note*: The registrar may specify an allotted time that all nonconformances must be corrected before he or she returns to re-audit.

Continued on next page

Achieving certification

You cannot fail certification. The worst that can happen is that you quit!

Appendix

Introduction	The pages within this appendix are examples of the ISO levels of documentation.
Background	These are actual pages documenting a certified quality system. The section of Document Control is discussed in the following pages.
Permission to distribute	ACT Manufacturing, Inc., has given permission to Information Mapping to copy and distribute the pages within this appendix.
In this appendix	This appendix includes examples of documents at the following levels: • Level A, • Level B, and • Level C.

4.4 Document Control

Policy

ACT establishes and maintains procedures to control all documents related to our ISO 9002 quality system and to control the production of our product.

Purpose

This element ensures our customers that our people have up-to-date documents concerning their product and our processes, and that we control changes to these documents.

Responsibility

Document Control is responsible for establishing and maintaining our documentation control system. Our managers and supervisors are responsible for ensuring that their people have current copies of the documents they need to perform their work, and for promptly removing out-of-date documents from the workplace.

Review and approval

We assign people who are familiar with the subject matter of a given document to review and approve new documents before we release them. Also, we assign people who are familiar with the original document to review and approve changes to the document.

We let receivers know as much as we can about the nature of the change and give them access to the information they need to make informed decisions.

Availability

Controlled copies of documents are available to our people as required.

Master list

Documentation Control maintains a master list that shows the current revision levels of customer documents and the current issue levels of documents related to our quality system so that our people know if they are using the correct document.

Continued on next page

4.4 Document Control, Continued

Review and re-issue	We re-issue documents after we make a significant number of changes. This number varies as a function of the extent and importance of the change.

Supporting documentation	The following is the list of documents that supports this quality system element:

4.4.000, Review and Approval of Quality System Documents

4.4.100, Master List

4.4.200, Control of Documents

4.4.300, Changes and Modifications

4.4.400, Review and Re-issue of Quality System Documents

Documentation Changes and Modifications

Introduction

This procedure is ACT's plan for changes and modifications to ensure compliance with Section 4.4 of the ACT Quality Manual concerning control of changes to documents to ensure traceability of issues.

Scope and purpose

This procedure provides a standardized approach to changes and modifications to all quality system documents, customer documents, and assembly work instructions.

Quality system and customer changes

Implementation of changes to quality system documents and customer documents are processed using an Engineering Change Order Process Flow Procedure as detailed in document 4.4.301.

Modifications

Implementation of one-time-only internal and related customer modifications are processed using a Manufacturing Deviation as detailed in document 4.4.305.

Assembly instruction changes

Implementation of changes concerning assembly work instruction changes, that do not adversely affect product quality of delivery, are processed using a Process Change Request as detailed on documents 4.8.803I and 4.8.508I.

Supporting documentation

The following is a list of documents to support this procedure:

4.4.301,   Engineering Change Order Process Flow

4.4.305,   Processing a Manufacturing Deviation

4.8.803I, Process Change Request

4.8.508II, Manufacturing Engineering Process Modification

Continued on next page

Documentation Changes and Modifications,
Continued

**Issue number
history**

The following is the issue number history for this procedure:

Issue #	ECO #	Date	Description	Originator
Pre	-	07/14/93	Preliminary Release	B. Gaumond
01	1109II	07/26/93	Release	B. Gaumond
02	1584II	09/14/93	delete 4.4.306, add 4.8.803I and 4.8.508II	F. Gormley

How to Inquire About Revision or Issue Levels

Introduction

This instruction is about how to use the GrowthPower system to inquire about the

- revisions of customer assemblies,
- revision of customer documents,
- issue level of ACT quality system documents, and
- issue level of assembly instructions.

Scope and purpose

This instruction concerns inquiry about customer revision levels or ACT issue levels.

How to inquire— customer revision or ACT document issue

This table shows how to inquire about customer revision levels or ACT quality system document issue levels.

Step	Action
1	Log onto GrowthPower.
2	Type "FM" at the colon prompt.
3	Select "Manufacturing" from the Main Menu.
4	Select "Inquiry" from the Manufacturing Menu.
5	Select "Parts" from the Inquiry menu.
6	Type the quality system document or assembly number of inquiry.
7	Select "Other Part Information" from the menu.
8	Follow the table below to view revision or issue levels.

IF you inquire on a ...	THEN view ...
document or form related to the quality system,	the "Engineering Status" for the current issue level.
customer assembly number,	the "Revision Level" for current revision level.

Continued on next page

How to Inquire About Revision or Issue Levels, Continued

How to inquire— customer document or ACT assembly instruction

This table shows how to inquire about customer document revision levels or ACT assembly instruction issue levels.

Step	Action
1	Log onto GrowthPower.
2	Type "FM" at the colon prompt.
3	Select "Manufacturing" from the Main Menu.
4	Select "Inquiry" from the Manufacturing Menu.
5	Select "Parts" from the Inquiry Menu.
6	Type the customer assembly number.
7	Select "Comments" from the menu.
8	View customer documents revision levels or assembly instruction issue levels.

Training method

The following is the training method for this work instruction:

Informal on-the-job training.

Supporting documents

The following are the documents to support this work instruction:

N/A

Issue number history

The following is the issue number history for this work instruction:

Issue #	ECO #	Date	Description	Originator
Pre	-	07/10/93	Preliminary Release	W. McDonald
01	1045II	07/26/93	Release	W. McDonald
02	1594II	09/17/93	Add training method	N. Kristiansen

Engineering Change Order Form

Form example The following is an example of the Engineering Change Order Form:

ACT manufacturing	**ENGINEERING CHANGE**		**Page Number**	**ECR/ECO Number**
Affects (circle one): ACTI ACTII ACTIII	Request ❑	Order ❑	1 of _____	
Originator:	Date:		Assembly/Document Number:	
Customer Name/Document Name:			Customer ECO #:	Cur Rev/Issue #:

TYPE OF CHANGE (check one):		PRIORITY OF REQUEST/CHANGE:	
NEW RELEASE		URGENT—CHANGE MUST BE MADE PRIOR TO FURTHER PROCESSING	
CHANGE or REVISION		ROUTINE—IMPLEMENT RUNNING CHANGE AT EARLIEST CONVENIENCE	
OBSOLESCENCE		ROUTINE—FOR ALL PRODUCTION AFTER:	
CLERICAL		OTHER (Explain).	
CORRECTION			

DESCRIPTION OF CHANGE (Attach separate sheet if necessary)

CUSTOMER NOTIFICATION REQUIRED?	CUSTOMER RESPONSE	
YES ❑ NO ❑		

SALES ORDERS AFFECTED			WORK ORDERS AFFECTED		
order #	quantity	ship date	order #	quantity	location

SIGNATURE ACKNOWLEDGEMENTS/APPROVALS

DEPARTMENT	DATE	DEPARTMENT	DATE

KEY DATES

Release date:	Effectivity date:	Check date:	Completion date:

Index

Index, Continued